Acclaim for Amelia Island
and
A Savory Place

"Take one part Victorian elegance, two parts laid-back island living attitude,

throw in some marine life (sea turtles and manatees galore), add a dash of southern

charm and a pinch of country-club flavor, and the result is Amelia Island.

The streets are lined with Queen Anne–style houses and enormous live oak trees,

and the vibe is both romantic and fanciful. Walking around the old district

made me feel like I was in the middle of a scene from an illustrated storybook."

Excerpt from *Getting a Grip* by Monica Seles
Avery, a member of Penguin Group (USA) Inc.

"What a treat this cookbook is! It contains such memorable photography

of Amelia Island that you may prefer to place it on the coffee table rather than

on the cookbook shelf. Yet it is overflowing with prized recipes shared

generously by the ladies of Amelia, who are masters at gracious entertaining.

And, most of all, it is all for such a worthy cause—Micah's Place,

a safe haven for victims of domestic violence."

C. Brett Carter
Well-known owner of two popular Amelia Island restaurants, caterer, and designer

A Savory Place

Culinary Favorites
of
Amelia Island

Micah's Place

A Collection of Recipes by the Micah's Place Auxiliary

All proceeds go to Micah's Place, a shelter for victims of domestic violence

A Savory Place

Culinary Favorites of Amelia Island

Published by Micah's Place

Copyright © 2010 by Micah's Place
P.O. Box 16287
Fernandina Beach, Florida 32035
904-491-6364

Photography © by Micah's Place

This cookbook is a collection of favorite recipes,
which are not necessarily original recipes.

ISBN: 978-0-615-29646-3

Edited, Designed, and Produced by
CommunityClassics®
an imprint of

FRP®INC

a wholly owned subsidiary of Southwestern/Great American, Inc.
P.O. Box 305142
Nashville, Tennessee 37230
800-358-0560

Manufactured in the United States of America
First Printing: 2010
4,000 copies

Table of Contents

History of Micah's Place

The vision of a domestic violence shelter and support program for victims of abuse in Nassau County, Florida, began in 1999. Initiated and led by the local Volunteer Center, Sheriff's Office, Clerk of Courts, and State's Attorney's Office, it was assisted by many community volunteers. This vision became a reality when Micah's Place was incorporated in 2000 and registered as a 501(c)(3) nonprofit organization.

The Auxiliary was formed in 2001 by a small group of women interested in supporting the efforts and programs of Micah's Place. There are now hundreds of women who undertake fund-raising projects, such as luncheons, galas, and the annual Home & Garden Tour, their signature event begun in 2003.

In 2003, Micah's Place opened a sixteen-bed emergency home and shelter and was fully certified by the Department of Children and Families that same year. The Purple Dove Resale Center was opened in 2008 to increase community visibility and raise additional funds. The Center assists families by providing the basic necessities incurred when establishing new lives and new homes.

Today, Micah's Place offers shelter and support, outreach services, court advocacy, education and prevention programs for youth and adults, and a twenty-four-hour toll-free hot line year-round.

Micah's Place was created in order to make a difference in our community. There is no definitive way to measure the value of a life—a woman or child saved—because the services of Micah's Place were available to them.

Our **Vision** is to end domestic violence one relationship at a time.

Dedication

We dedicate this cookbook to

Marilyn Evans-Jones

President Emeritus
Micah's Place Board of Directors

Marilyn's devotion and concern were a constant force
from the beginning. She was instrumental in
securing land for our shelter, recruiting early volunteers,
and raising necessary funds. As a Florida
State Representative, Marilyn also supported issues
to protect victims of domestic violence.
She remains an inspiration to all.

Many people were involved in this conception of
a safe place for victims of domestic violence.
We value all of the volunteers whose vision and
enthusiasm made Micah's Place a reality.

History of Amelia Island

Amelia Island is the only community in the United States to have experienced life under eight different flags. The island and its charming seaport village of Fernandina Beach are largely characterized by its colorful past. Timucuans, pirates, shrimpers, royalty, and the rich have inhabited Florida's northeastern shores for more than 4,000 years.

Artifacts from the mid-sixteenth century indicate the struggle over the island's thirteen-mile stretch of coastal land. Our maritime heritage is due primarily to the deepest natural harbor on North America's coast prior to dredging. The harbor provided easy access for smugglers, pirates, and sea captains.

As early as 2500 B.C., the Timucuans inhabited our island. The first European visitors were the French in 1562 who raised the first of our eight flags. The Spanish defeated the French in 1565 and were in control for almost two hundred years.

The English arrived in 1763 and named the island in honor of Princess Amelia, King George II's daughter. There is a saying, "The French visited, the Spanish developed, the English named, and the Americans tamed." Over the years, rebel forces raised several other flags until the United States took possession in 1821 and statehood was granted in 1845.

The railroad brought to Fernandina Beach a glorious Golden Age. In the late nineteenth century the island became an import-export center and tourist mecca. During the early twentieth century Fernandina Beach became known as the birthplace of the modern shrimping industry.

Fernandina Beach is cited on the National Register of Historic Places for its preservation of late Victorian architecture. In recent times the island has gained national recognition as a desirable resort destination.

Amelia Island Photography

Front Cover Image

Mount Hope Plantation is the oldest home on Amelia Island and is located toward the south end of the island. The original structure was built in 1797 but was burned by Union troops in 1862. As an indigo and Sea Island cotton plantation, the original Georgian-style farmhouse, now in just its third ownership, has been restored to perfection with historical accuracy. The wide verandas on both sides of the house capture the island breezes, and the widow's walk offers a spectacular panoramic view of the ocean and the marsh. Mount Hope is one of only a small number of plantation-style homes in Florida and is an architectural gem of the past that we treasure and admire.

Front Page Image

Towering live oaks, dripping with Spanish moss, are a signature of our island. In time, their widespread branches bend and intertwine, forming a forest archway over the street. Designated as a canopy road, signs request drivers to slow down and enjoy their majestic formation. Overhead flashes of blue sky may be seen, creating a breathtaking cool oasis that never fails to delight and welcome us. These live oaks grow fifty feet tall, and their tough wood was used for shipbuilding. They are one of the most beautiful shade trees in Florida.

Back Cover Image

As we look through the vista created by a gigantic oak, we never fail to marvel at the vastness of our protected marshes. A unique representation of Florida coastal landscape, their colors are ever changing with the seasons, the months, and even the hours. The Amelia River meanders between the dock at Mount Hope Plantation and the marsh. Extending all the way to the Intracoastal Waterway, the marshes with their exceptional beauty provide a safe habitat for an extensive array of fish, water birds, and wildlife.

Beginnings

As the sun peeks over the ocean, we capture this unique early morning moment
that is dawn. Rising quickly, the amazing color delights both shell seekers and sun
seekers, young and old. The never-ending waves and this quiet time of day
create the magical balance of sun, sky, and sea. It is the perfect beginning of our day.

Bacon and Cheese Gougères

1/2 cup water
1/4 cup (1/2 stick) butter, softened
1/8 teaspoon salt
1/8 teaspoon black pepper
1/8 teaspoon red pepper
1/2 cup all-purpose flour
2 eggs
1/3 cup shredded Gruyère cheese
1 tablespoon finely grated Parmesan cheese
1/2 teaspoon Dijon mustard
1/4 teaspoon dry mustard
12 slices bacon, crisp-cooked and crumbled
2 tablespoons finely chopped green onions
1/4 teaspoon paprika
1 ounce arugula for garnish

Bring the water, butter, salt, black pepper and red pepper to a boil in a large saucepan. Add the flour and stir vigorously. Cook until the mixture forms a ball, stirring constantly. Remove from the heat. Add the eggs one at a time, beating well after each addition. Stir in the Gruyère cheese, Parmesan cheese, Dijon mustard, dry mustard, bacon and green onions. Drop the dough by teaspoonfuls onto a buttered baking sheet. Bake at 400 degrees for 17 to 20 minutes or until the centers are tender and moist when opened but not mushy. Remove from the oven and sprinkle with the paprika. Garnish the gougères with the arugula. **Serves 8.**

The baked gougères can be cooled and placed in an airtight container. Freeze for up to one month. To serve, place the frozen gougères on an ungreased baking sheet and bake at 350 degrees for 20 minutes or until warm.

Barbecue Bean Salsa

1 (28-ounce) can diced tomatoes
1 (6-ounce) can vegetarian
  baked beans
1 small red onion, chopped
1/2 bunch cilantro, chopped
Juice of 1 lemon

1/4 cup barbecue sauce
3 garlic cloves, minced
1 (4-ounce) can diced green
  chiles, drained
1 tablespoon honey
2 tablespoons mild picante sauce

Drain the tomatoes and beans, reserving the liquid. Combine the tomatoes, beans, onion, cilantro, lemon juice, barbecue sauce, garlic, green chiles, honey and picante sauce in a bowl and mix well. Add the reserved liquid if needed for the desired consistency. Spoon into a serving bowl. Serve with Fritos Scoops. **Serves 14 to 16.**

Black Bean Hummus

2 (15-ounce) cans black beans
3/4 cup tahini (sesame
  seed paste)
1/4 cup fresh lemon juice
1/4 cup packed chopped
  fresh cilantro
4 green onions, sliced

2 tablespoons olive oil
2 garlic cloves, minced
1/2 teaspoon ground cumin
1/2 teaspoon chili powder
1/2 teaspoon cayenne pepper
Salt to taste
Black pepper to taste

Drain the beans and rinse well. Process the beans, tahini, lemon juice, cilantro, green onions, olive oil, garlic, cumin, chili powder and cayenne pepper in a food processor until smooth. Add the salt and black pepper and mix well. Spoon into a serving bowl and serve with pita bread triangles. **Serves 10 to 12.**

Black Bean Hummus is also great served with
fresh vegetables for dipping.

Blue Cheese Bites

8 ounces cream cheese, softened
1 cup crumbled blue cheese
2/3 cup chopped pecans
Pears, thinly sliced
Lemon juice
Belgian endive leaves

Combine the cream cheese, blue cheese and pecans in a bowl and mix well. Brush pear slices with lemon juice. Spoon 1 teaspoon of the cream cheese mixture onto each endive leaf and top each with a pear slice. Arrange on a serving platter. **Serves 4 to 6.**

Grape tomato halves may be used instead of the pear slices.
The spread can be served with crackers.

Chipped Beef Cheese Spread

1 (4-ounce) jar chipped beef
16 ounces cream cheese, softened
1 tablespoon mayonnaise
1 teaspoon lemon juice
7 green onions, chopped
Garlic salt to taste
Chopped pecans, toasted

Rinse and drain the beef. Chop the beef and set aside. Combine the chopped beef, cream cheese, mayonnaise, lemon juice, green onions and garlic salt in a bowl and mix well. Shape into a ball and roll in pecans. Wrap in plastic wrap and chill for 24 hours. To serve, unwrap and place in the center of a serving platter. Surround with assorted crackers. **Serves 10 to 12.**

A must for your next party.

Coconut Chicken Balls

8 ounces cream cheese, softened
1 cup finely chopped cooked chicken
1 cup slivered almonds, finely ground
2 tablespoons mayonnaise
1 tablespoon curry powder
2 to 3 tablespoons chopped chutney
1/2 teaspoon Lawry's seasoned salt
Grated coconut

Combine the cream cheese, chicken, almonds, mayonnaise, curry powder, chutney and seasoned salt in a bowl and mix well. Chill, covered, in the refrigerator. Shape into small balls and roll in the coconut. Chill until serving time. Arrange on a serving plate with wooden picks for serving. **Makes 3 dozen.**

Always a favorite.

Deviled Green Eggs and Bacon

1/4 cup frozen chopped spinach
6 hard-cooked eggs
2 tablespoons mayonnaise
4 slices bacon, crisp-cooked and crumbled
1 tablespoon apple cider vinegar
1 tablespoon butter, softened
11/2 teaspoons sugar
1/4 teaspoon salt
1/4 teaspoon pepper

Thaw the spinach and squeeze dry. Peel the eggs and cut into halves lengthwise. Mash the egg yolks in a bowl. Add the spinach, mayonnaise, bacon, vinegar, butter, sugar, salt and pepper and mix well. Spoon into the egg whites and place on a serving platter. **Serves 12.**

A great variation on the original. For ease of preparation, microwave bacon can be used and crumbled in the cooking pouch.

Endive with Goat Cheese

10 ounces goat cheese
1 tablespoon olive oil
1 teaspoon grated lemon zest
1^1/$_2$ teaspoons fresh lemon juice
1^1/$_2$ tablespoons chopped fresh cilantro
1^1/$_2$ tablespoons chopped fresh chives
^{1}/$_8$ teaspoon salt
^{1}/$_8$ teaspoon pepper
30 Belgian endive leaves (about 4 heads)
15 grape tomatoes, cut into halves
30 cilantro leaves for garnish

Process the cheese, olive oil, lemon zest and lemon juice in a food processor until smooth. Spoon into a small bowl. Stir in the chopped cilantro, chives, salt and pepper. Mound 1^1/$_2$ teaspoons of the cheese mixture onto each endive leaf and top with a tomato half. Garnish each with a cilantro leaf. Place on a serving platter. Chill, covered, for up to 1 day. **Makes 30 appetizers.**

Boursin cheese may be used instead of goat cheese.

Feta Cheese Spread

^{1}/$_2$ cup crumbled feta cheese
4 ounces cream cheese, softened
^{1}/$_3$ cup mayonnaise
1 garlic clove, minced
^{1}/$_4$ teaspoon basil
^{1}/$_4$ teaspoon oregano
^{1}/$_8$ teaspoon dill weed
^{1}/$_8$ teaspoon thyme

Process the feta cheese, cream cheese, mayonnaise, garlic, basil, oregano, dill weed and thyme in a food processor until well mixed. Serve with crackers or vegetables. **Serves 10.**

Fruit and Cheese Spread

8 ounces cream cheese, softened
1 cup pineapple preserves
6 ounces Swiss cheese, shredded
1/2 cup dried cranberries
1 cup pecans, chopped and divided
2 tablespoons dry sherry

Combine the cream cheese, preserves, Swiss cheese, dried cranberries, 1/2 cup of the pecans and the sherry in a bowl and mix well. Spread in an ungreased 9-inch pie plate. Sprinkle with the remaining 1/2 cup pecans. Bake at 375 degrees for 14 to 16 minutes or until softened. Serve with apple slices, pear slices or crackers. **Serves 14.**

The spread can be made one day in advance and can be frozen.

Hot Buffalo Chicken Dip

8 ounces cream cheese, softened
2 to 3 cups shredded cooked chicken
1/2 cup medium-hot Buffalo wing sauce
1/2 cup chunky blue cheese salad dressing
1/2 cup (2 ounces) shredded mozzarella cheese

Spread the cream cheese over the bottom of an 8×8-inch baking dish or 8-inch pie plate. Combine the chicken and wing sauce in a bowl and mix well. Spread over the cream cheese layer. Spread the salad dressing over the chicken mixture. Top with the mozzarella cheese. Bake at 350 degrees for 20 minutes. Serve with Tostitos or Fritos Scoops. **Serves 8.**

Substitute blue cheese crumbles for the salad dressing, if desired.

Layered Pesto Cheese Loaf

1 **cup fresh spinach leaves**
3/4 **cup fresh flat-leaf parsley**
1/4 **cup fresh basil leaves**
1 **teaspoon minced garlic**
1/4 **cup olive oil**
1/4 **cup finely chopped walnuts**
1 **cup (4 ounces) grated Parmesan cheese**
8 **ounces cream cheese, softened**
4 **ounces Roquefort cheese, softened**
1/4 **cup slivered sun-dried tomatoes, patted dry**

Line a 2 1/2×5 1/2-inch loaf pan with plastic wrap, leaving enough extending over the sides to cover the top. Rinse the spinach and pat dry. Place the spinach, parsley, basil and garlic in a food processor. Add the olive oil gradually, processing constantly until the mixture is smooth. Spoon into a bowl. Add the walnuts and Parmesan cheese and mix well.

Mix the cream cheese and Roquefort cheese in a bowl until smooth. Spread one-third of the cream cheese mixture over the bottom of the prepared pan. Layer the pesto mixture, sun-dried tomatoes and remaining cheese mixture one-half at a time over the cheese layer, ending with the cream cheese mixture. Cover with the overhanging plastic wrap. Chill for 24 hours. Remove from the refrigerator and let stand for 30 minutes. Invert onto a serving platter and remove the plastic wrap. Serve with crackers. **Serves 12.**

To save time, use an 8-ounce jar of basil pesto. Pine nuts or pecans may be used instead of the walnuts. A mild Gorgonzola cheese may be used for the Roquefort cheese.

Lemon Shrimp

1/2 cup fresh lemon juice
1/4 cup vegetable oil
1 garlic clove, minced
1 tablespoon dry mustard
1 teaspoon salt
1/4 teaspoon pepper
2 pounds large shrimp, peeled and deveined
1 onion, thinly sliced
2 tablespoons chopped pimento
1/4 cup chopped parsley
1 lemon, thinly sliced, for garnish

Combine the lemon juice, oil, garlic, dry mustard, salt and pepper in a bowl and mix well. Pour one-half of the dressing over the shrimp in a bowl and toss to coat well. Chill, covered, for 2 hours or longer, stirring once or twice. Place the shrimp in a single layer on a baking sheet. Bake at 450 degrees for 8 to 10 minutes or until the shrimp turn pink. Arrange on a serving platter. Add the onion, pimento and parsley to the remaining dressing and mix well. Sprinkle over the shrimp. Garnish with the lemon slices. **Serves 10.**

*Always a hit with the men! For another presentation,
thread two cooked shrimp on each wooden skewer and then sprinkle
with the dressing. Shrimp may be served on Bibb lettuce
as a first course for six to eight people.*

Mediterranean Eggplant

2 tablespoons olive oil
1 onion, chopped
1 green bell pepper, chopped
1 eggplant, peeled and chopped
1/2 cup sun-dried tomatoes,
cut into strips
1 carrot, shredded
1 teaspoon salt
1/4 teaspoon pepper
1 teaspoon sugar
1 teaspoon red wine vinegar
2 tablespoons finely chopped cilantro
Pita bread rounds, cut into 6 or 8 wedges

Heat the olive oil in a large skillet. Add the onion and sauté for 2 to 3 minutes or until soft. Stir in the bell pepper, eggplant, sun-dried tomatoes, carrot, salt, pepper, sugar and vinegar. Simmer for 15 to 20 minutes or until the vegetables are tender, stirring occasionally. Stir in the cilantro. Spoon into a serving bowl and surround with the pita bread wedges. **Serves 6 to 8.**

Miniature Shrimp Burgers

2 pounds uncooked medium shrimp, peeled and deveined
3/4 cup mayonnaise, divided
1 Vidalia onion, minced
1 teaspoon Worcestershire sauce
Pinch of cayenne pepper
Kosher salt and black pepper to taste
1 cup panko
Olive oil for sautéing
1/4 cup chili sauce
Tabasco sauce to taste
Bibb lettuce leaves

Finely chop the shrimp and place in a large bowl. Add 1/4 cup of the mayonnaise, the onion and Worcestershire sauce and mix well. Stir in the cayenne pepper, kosher salt and black pepper. Shape into miniature patties. Dredge in the bread crumbs and place on a baking sheet. Chill, covered with plastic wrap, for 4 to 5 hours. Sauté the patties in olive oil in a skillet over medium heat for 3 minutes on each side or until crisp and golden brown. Drain and set aside. Combine the remaining 1/2 cup mayonnaise, the chili sauce and Tabasco sauce in a bowl and mix well. To serve, place each shrimp patty on a Bibb lettuce leaf and top with a dollop of the chili mayonnaise. **Makes 20 to 24 miniature burgers.**

Prosciutto-Wrapped Apple Bites

1 or 2 Gala apples
Lemon juice for sprinkling
4 paper-thin slices prosciutto
1 1/2 cups loosely packed arugula
1 ounce package fresh basil
1/4 teaspoon coarsely
   ground pepper

Cut the unpeeled apples into 1/4- to 1/2-inch slices about 3 inches long. Sprinkle with lemon juice to prevent browning. Cut each prosciutto slice lengthwise into four strips. Place one apple slice on top of two arugula leaves and one basil leaf. Wrap each with a prosciutto strip. Arrange on a serving platter and sprinkle with the pepper. **Serves 8.**

The pepper makes this fabulous! Small melon slices may be used instead of the apple slices. To make ahead, prepare the recipe as directed and cover with damp paper towels. Chill for 30 minutes before serving.

Puff Pastry Gruyère Pinwheels

1 (10-ounce) package frozen chopped spinach
1/4 cup (1/2 stick) butter, softened and divided
1 cup sliced fresh mushrooms
4 ounces Gruyère cheese, grated
1 teaspoon garlic powder (optional)
1 (17-ounce) package frozen puff pastry, thawed

Thaw the spinach and squeeze dry. Melt 2 tablespoons of the butter in a skillet over medium heat. Add the mushrooms and sauté for 5 minutes. Combine the spinach, sautéed mushrooms, cheese and garlic powder in a bowl and mix well. Roll the pastry sheets into 11×13-inch rectangles, pressing the seams together. Melt the remaining 2 tablespoons butter in a saucepan. Brush the pastry rectangles with the melted butter and spread the spinach mixture over the top. Roll up to enclose the filling, beginning with the long side. Wrap in plastic wrap and chill for up to 2 days. Cut the pastry rolls into slices 1/4 inch thick and place on a baking sheet lined with baking parchment. Bake at 350 degrees for 15 to 20 minutes or until light brown.

Variation: For **Puff Pastry Artichoke Pinwheels,** combine one 10-ounce package frozen chopped spinach, thawed and squeezed dry, one 14-ounce jar marinated artichoke hearts, drained and chopped, 1/2 cup mayonnaise, 1/2 cup (2 ounces) grated Parmesan cheese, garlic powder to taste, onion powder to taste, salt and pepper to taste in a bowl and mix well. Proceed with the recipe as directed above. **Serves 8.**

These are great to have in the freezer for guests. Wrap the
pastry rolls in foil and freeze for up to three months. Thaw and proceed
with the recipe as directed.

Reuben Dip

1 (16-ounce) jar sauerkraut, drained
1 (4-ounce) jar dried beef, chopped
3/4 cup mayonnaise
1 cup (4 ounces) shredded Swiss cheese

Combine the sauerkraut, dried beef, mayonnaise and cheese in a bowl and mix well. Spoon into a small baking dish. Bake at 350 degrees for 20 minutes or until heated through. Serve with rye Triscuits or Fritos Scoops. **Serves 4 to 6.**

Very simple and scrumptious.

Roasted Pepper and Artichoke Dip

1 (7-ounce) jar roasted red peppers, drained
1 (6-ounce) jar marinated artichoke hearts, drained
1/2 cup parsley
1/3 cup olive oil
4 garlic cloves
1 tablespoon lemon juice
1/2 cup (2 ounces) Parmigiano-Reggiano cheese
Salt and pepper to taste

Process the red peppers, artichoke hearts, parsley, olive oil, garlic, lemon juice, cheese, salt and pepper in a food processor until blended. Spoon into a serving bowl. Chill, covered, until serving time. Serve with toasted French bread or Panetini. **Serves 8.**

A great tapenade.

Shrimp Butter

1¹/₄ pounds large shrimp, cooked, peeled and deveined
6 green onions, chopped
3 tablespoons chopped fresh chives
1 tablespoon fresh dill weed
¹/₂ teaspoon salt
Pepper to taste
3 tablespoons butter, softened
¹/₂ cup heavy cream
1 tablespoon dry vermouth

Reserve several of the shrimp for garnish. Process the remaining shrimp, the green onions, chives, dill weed, salt, pepper, butter, cream and vermouth in a food processor until smooth. Spoon into a crock or serving bowl. Chill, covered, for 4 hours. Garnish with the reserved shrimp. Serve with assorted crackers. **Serves 4 to 6.**

This recipe can be prepared without using a food processor. Finely chop the shrimp and mix with the remaining ingredients.

Spinach Mold

2 (10-ounce) packages frozen chopped spinach, thawed
2 ribs celery
2 green onions
2 garlic cloves
1¹/₄ cups mayonnaise
¹/₂ envelope unflavored gelatin
1 teaspoon salt, or to taste
Pepper to taste

Cook the spinach using the package directions. Drain the spinach and squeeze dry. Process the celery, green onions and garlic in a food processor until chopped. Add the spinach, mayonnaise, gelatin, salt and pepper and blend well. Pour into an oiled serving bowl. Chill for 2 hours. Invert onto a serving plate and unmold. Surround with vegetables or crackers to serve. **Serves 12.**

For a fancy presentation, frost with sour cream after unmolding.

Swedish Meatballs

4 slices dry white bread, trimmed
1¼ cups finely chopped onions, divided
1 egg
¼ teaspoon freshly grated nutmeg
1 teaspoon ground allspice
1 teaspoon salt
½ teaspoon pepper
1¾ pounds ground turkey
1 teaspoon vegetable oil
3 tablespoons sherry
3 cups beef broth, divided
2½ tablespoons cornstarch
1 tablespoon Worcestershire sauce
1 tablespoon sour cream
2 tablespoons chopped fresh dill weed

Process the bread in a food processor until fine crumbs form. Mix the bread crumbs and ¾ cup of the onions in a bowl. Whisk the egg, nutmeg, allspice, salt and pepper in a small bowl. Add to the crumb mixture. Add the turkey and mix just until combined. Shape into small balls less than 1 inch in diameter. Heat the oil in a nonstick skillet over medium heat. Add the meatballs and cook until brown. Remove the meatballs with a slotted spoon to a shallow baking dish and cover tightly, reserving the drippings in the skillet. Bake the meatballs at 375 degrees for 20 minutes or until the meatballs are just cooked through.

Add the sherry and the remaining ½ cup onions to the reserved drippings in the skillet, stirring to scrape up the brown bits from the bottom of the skillet. Simmer until most of the liquid evaporates. Add 2½ cups of the broth. Bring to a boil. Whisk the cornstarch and the remaining ½ cup broth in a small bowl. Stir into the hot broth mixture. Boil for 1 minute or until thickened, stirring constantly. Remove from the heat. Stir in the Worcestershire sauce, sour cream and dill weed. Place the meatballs in a chafing dish and cover with some of the sauce. Serve immediately with wooden picks for serving. **Serves 12.**

*The meatballs can be prepared one day ahead and chilled, covered,
until ready to brown. This dish may also be served over noodles
as an entrée because there will be enough sauce.*

Turkey Pâté

2 cups coarsely chopped cooked turkey breast
1/4 cup sliced green onions
1/2 cup sour cream
1/4 cup mango chutney
1/2 teaspoon curry powder
1 tablespoon chopped fresh parsley

Line a small bowl with plastic wrap, extending over the side to cover the top. Process the turkey, green onions, sour cream, chutney and curry powder in a food processor until smooth. Spoon into the prepared bowl and cover with the plastic wrap, pressing to pack down. Chill for 2 hours. Uncover and invert onto a serving platter. Remove the plastic wrap. Sprinkle with the parsley. Serve with crackers. **Serves 8 to 10.**

Wild Mushroom Sauté

1 1/2 tablespoons butter
1 tablespoon olive oil
1/4 cup minced shallots
1 garlic clove, minced
1 pound wild mushrooms, sliced
1 teaspoon minced fresh thyme, divided
1/4 cup dry white wine
1/4 cup heavy cream
2 tablespoons minced fresh chives, divided
Salt and pepper to taste
Pita chips

Melt the butter with the olive oil in a large skillet. Add the shallots and garlic and sauté for 2 minutes. Add the mushrooms and 1/2 teaspoon of the thyme. Sauté for 15 minutes or until golden brown. Add the wine. Boil for 2 minutes or until the liquid evaporates. Stir in the cream, 1 tablespoon of the chives and the remaining 1/2 teaspoon thyme. Simmer for 1 minute. Add salt, pepper and the remaining 1 tablespoon chives. Place a dollop of the mushroom mixture onto each toasted pita bread and serve. **Serves 8.**

*Use different kinds of mushrooms in this recipe such as
crimini, oyster mushrooms, and stemmed shiitake.*

Brunch
& Breads

The beauty and tranquility of Amelia Island's white beaches stretch along thirteen miles of coastline. Protected sea oats wave gracefully in the breeze and help prevent erosion because of their extensive root system. The constantly changing dunes and the blue-washed sky provide the perfect background for a walk on the beach.

Apple Cranberry Delight

3 cups unpeeled Granny Smith apple chunks
1 pound fresh cranberries
1½ cups granulated sugar
1½ cups quick-cooking oats
¾ cup packed brown sugar
⅓ cup all-purpose flour
1 cup chopped pecans
2 cups (4 sticks) butter, melted

Place the apples and cranberries in a 9×13-inch baking dish. Sprinkle with the granulated sugar. Mix the oats, brown sugar, flour and pecans in a bowl. Spread over the fruit. Drizzle the butter over the top. Bake at 325 degrees for 35 minutes. **Serves 10.**

Breakfast Pizza

1 pound bulk pork sausage
1 (8-count) can refrigerator crescent rolls
3 or 4 eggs, at room temperature
¼ cup milk
½ teaspoon salt
⅛ teaspoon pepper
1 cup frozen hash brown potatoes, thawed
1 cup (4 ounces) shredded sharp Cheddar cheese
2 tablespoons grated Parmesan cheese

Brown the sausage in a skillet, stirring until crumbly. Drain and set aside. Unroll the crescent roll dough. Press into a circle in a pizza pan. Bake at 375 degrees on the lowest oven rack for 8 minutes or until the crust is puffy. Remove from the oven. Reduce the oven temperature to 350 degrees. Beat the eggs, milk, salt and pepper in a bowl. Sprinkle with the sausage, potatoes and Cheddar cheese. Pour the egg mixture over the top. Sprinkle with the Parmesan cheese. Bake on the lowest oven rack for 20 to 25 minutes or until the crust is golden brown. Cut into wedges to serve. **Serves 4.**

Copper Mountain Quiche

1 pound fresh spinach	1/2 cup mayonnaise
2 tablespoons all-purpose flour	1/2 cup cream
1 cup (4 ounces) shredded Cheddar cheese	10 slices bacon, crisp-cooked and crumbled
1 cup (4 ounces) shredded Swiss cheese	8 ounces fresh mushrooms, sliced
3 eggs, beaten	1 bunch green onions, sliced
	1 unbaked (9-inch) pie shell

Rinse and trim the spinach. Cook the spinach in a small amount of water in a saucepan just until tender. Drain well and chop. Combine the spinach and flour in a large bowl. Add the Cheddar cheese, Swiss cheese, eggs, mayonnaise, cream, bacon, mushrooms and green onions and mix well. Pour into the pie shell. Bake at 350 degrees for 1 hour or until set. **Serves 6 to 8.**

The quiche may be made without the crust and baked in a 9×9-inch baking dish. Cut into squares to serve. Frozen chopped spinach may be used instead of fresh spinach. Cook using the package directions; drain and squeeze dry. The quiche may be baked in advance. Cool and freeze. Thaw and bake until heated through.

Fruity Rice Salad

3 ounces cream cheese, softened	3 fresh peaches, chopped
1/2 cup plain yogurt	1 cup green grape halves
1/4 cup honey	1/2 cup sliced celery
2 tablespoons lemon juice	1/2 cup raisins or cranberries
1 teaspoon lemon zest	1/2 cup chopped pecans, toasted
2 cups cooked rice, cooled	

Beat the cream cheese, yogurt, honey, lemon juice and lemon zest in a bowl until smooth. Stir in the rice, peaches, grapes, celery and raisins. Chill, covered, for 6 hours or longer. Stir in the pecans just before serving. **Serves 6.**

One and one-half cups frozen sliced peaches, thawed and chopped, may be used for the fresh peaches. Fresh nectarines may also be used instead of the peaches.

Ham and Grits Quiche

1 unbaked (9-inch) deep-dish pie shell	1/4 teaspoon nutmeg
1/2 cup chopped fresh mushrooms	1 1/2 cups chopped cooked ham
1/4 cup chopped onion	1/2 cup (2 ounces) shredded Swiss cheese, divided
1 tablespoon butter	1/2 cup (2 ounces) shredded Cheddar cheese, divided
1 cup half-and-half	6 slices bacon, crisp-cooked and crumbled
4 eggs, beaten	1/2 cup quick-cooking grits, cooked
1/2 teaspoon dry mustard	
1/4 teaspoon pepper	

Bake the pie shell using the package directions. Sauté the mushrooms and onion in the butter in a skillet for 5 minutes or until tender. Remove from the heat and set aside. Combine the half-and-half, eggs, dry mustard, pepper and nutmeg in a bowl and mix well. Sprinkle the ham over the baked crust. Sprinkle with one-half of the Swiss cheese, one-half of the Cheddar cheese and the bacon. Spoon the mushroom mixture over the bacon. Spread the grits over the mushroom mixture. Sprinkle with the remaining Swiss cheese and Cheddar cheese. Pour the egg mixture over the cheese. Bake at 350 degrees for 40 to 45 minutes or until the center is set. Let stand at room temperature for 5 minutes before serving. **Serves 6.**

For variation, use Italian sausage that has been sautéed, drained, and crumbled in place of the ham.

Peaches with Red Wine Sauce

4 large peaches	2 cups fruity red wine
Corn oil for brushing	2 tablespoons brown sugar

Cut the peaches into halves and remove the pits. Brush each peach half with corn oil. Whisk the wine and brown sugar in a small bowl until blended. Place the peaches in a 9×13-inch baking dish. Pour the wine sauce over the peaches. Bake at 325 degrees for 20 to 25 minutes, basting with the sauce twice. Spoon a small amount of the wine sauce into shallow serving bowls. Add a peach half to each bowl and drizzle with more of the wine sauce. Serve warm or at room temperature. **Serves 8.**

Ripe Olive Quiche

Parmesan Pastry

1¼ cups sifted all-purpose flour

¼ cup yellow cornmeal

¼ cup (1 ounce) grated Parmesan cheese

¾ teaspoon salt

1/16 teaspoon cayenne pepper

½ cup shortening

3 to 4 tablespoons cold water

Quiche

6 slices bacon, cut into 1-inch pieces

4 eggs, beaten

¾ teaspoon salt

⅛ teaspoon white pepper

1 cup heavy cream

1 cup milk

¾ cup thinly sliced green onions

¼ cup (1 ounce) grated Parmesan cheese

1 tablespoon pimento strips

½ cup pitted ripe olives, cut into wedges

To prepare the pastry, mix the flour, cornmeal, cheese, salt and cayenne pepper in a bowl. Cut in the shortening until crumbly. Sprinkle with the water and mix to form a dough. Shape into a ball. Roll into a 12-inch circle on a floured board. Fit into a 10-inch pie plate, fluting the edge. Bake on the lower oven rack at 350 degree for 5 minutes. Remove from the oven and maintain the oven temperature.

To prepare the quiche, sauté the bacon in a skillet until crisp; drain well. Mix the eggs, salt and white pepper in a bowl. Stir in the cream and milk. Add the green onions, cheese, pimento, olives and bacon and mix well. Pour into the pie shell. Bake for 40 minutes. Let stand at room temperature for 10 minutes before serving. **Serves 8.**

Skillet Pancake

3 eggs	1/4 cup (1/2 stick) butter, softened
1/2 cup milk	and divided
1/3 cup all-purpose flour	1/4 cup sugar
1/4 teaspoon salt	1/4 teaspoon cinnamon
2 Granny Smith apples	Lemon juice to taste
2 tablespoons fresh lemon juice	

Beat the eggs, milk, flour and salt in a bowl until smooth. Let stand at room temperature for 1 hour. Peel the apples and cut into thin slices. Sprinkle with 2 tablespoons lemon juice to prevent browning. Melt 2 tablespoons of the butter in a 12-inch ovenproof skillet. Pour in the batter. Cover with the apple slices. Bake at 375 degrees for 10 to 15 minutes or until brown. Slide the pancake onto a serving plate. Spread with the remaining 2 tablespoons butter. Sprinkle with a mixture of the sugar and cinnamon. Drizzle with lemon juice to taste. **Serves 3 or 4.**

Smoked Salmon Frittata

8 eggs	2 teaspoons olive oil
1/2 cup milk	3 ounces cream cheese, chopped
1/4 cup chopped fresh chives	3 ounces thinly sliced smoked
1/4 cup chopped fresh basil	salmon, chopped
1/8 teaspoon salt	1 red onion, thinly sliced for
1/2 teaspoon pepper	garnish

Whisk the eggs, milk, chives, basil, salt and pepper in a bowl. Heat the olive oil in a 12-inch ovenproof skillet over medium heat. Add the egg mixture and scatter the cream cheese over the top. Cook until set on the bottom, lifting the edge to let the uncooked egg mixture flow underneath. Remove from the heat. Sprinkle the salmon over the top and press to allow the salmon to settle into the top. Bake at 425 degrees for 5 to 7 minutes or until set. Broil 6 inches from the heat source for 1 to 1 1/2 minutes or until slightly puffed and golden brown. Cool for 5 minutes. Loosen the edge from the side of the skillet and slide onto a serving plate. Cut into wedges and serve warm or at room temperature. Garnish with red onion, if desired. **Serves 4.**

Spiced Pineapple

1 fresh pineapple
2 tablespoons butter, melted
2 tablespoons bourbon or apple cider
1/4 cup packed brown sugar
1/2 teaspoon pepper

Peel and core the pineapple. Cut the pineapple lengthwise into four pieces. Cut each piece into 1/2-inch slices. Place in a lightly buttered 9×13-inch baking dish. Drizzle with the butter and bourbon. Sprinkle with the brown sugar and pepper. Bake at 350 degrees for 25 minutes. **Serves 6.**

Great to serve for brunch.

Spinach Pie with Muenster Crust

12 ounces Muenster cheese, sliced
3 (10-ounce) packages frozen chopped spinach
1 cup cottage cheese
3 eggs, beaten
1 small onion, chopped
1/3 cup grated Parmesan cheese
Salt and pepper to taste

Line an ungreased 9-inch pie plate with overlapping slices of the cheese, covering the bottom and reaching three-fourths of the way up the side. Cook the spinach using the package directions. Drain and squeeze dry. Combine the spinach, cottage cheese, eggs, onion, Parmesan cheese, salt and pepper in a bowl and mix well. Pour into the prepared pie plate. Bake at 350 degrees for 1 hour or until set. Let stand at room temperature for 5 minutes before serving. **Serves 8.**

Spring Frittata

8 asparagus spears, cut into 1-inch pieces
4 ounces fresh mushrooms, sliced
6 eggs, beaten
2 tablespoons milk
1 teaspoon minced fresh thyme
1 teaspoon minced fresh chives
1/4 teaspoon salt, or to taste
Pepper to taste
2 tablespoons butter
2 cups coarsely chopped arugula leaves
1/4 cup (1 ounce) shredded mozzarella cheese
2 tablespoons grated Parmesan cheese

Heat a stove-top grill pan until hot. Coat with nonstick olive oil spray. Add the asparagus and mushrooms. Grill for 5 minutes or until light brown on each side. Combine the eggs, milk, thyme, chives, salt and pepper in a bowl and mix well. Melt the butter in a large ovenproof skillet over medium heat. Add the arugula. Sauté for 1 minute or just until wilted. Add the egg mixture and stir lightly. Cook for 5 minutes or until set on the bottom and the top is still runny; do not stir. Sprinkle with the grilled vegetables, mozzarella cheese and Parmesan cheese. Broil for 3 to 4 minutes or until golden brown. Serve immediately. **Serves 4.**

Tomato Aspic with Shrimp

8 ounces cooked shrimp
2 tablespoons unflavored gelatin
1/2 cup water
1 (10-ounce) can tomato soup
9 ounces cream cheese
1 cup mayonnaise
1 cup chopped celery
1/4 cup chopped onion
1/4 cup chopped green bell pepper
Chopped red and yellow bell peppers to taste
Lettuce leaves

Peel the shrimp and devein. Chop the shrimp and set aside. Soften the gelatin in the water in a bowl. Heat the soup in a double boiler over boiling water. Add the cream cheese. Cook until smooth, stirring constantly. Stir in the gelatin mixture. Remove from the heat to cool. Add the mayonnaise, celery, onion, bell peppers and shrimp. Spoon into a 9×13-inch dish. Chill until set. Serve on lettuce-lined individual serving plates. **Serves 12.**

Blueberry Quick Bread

5 cups all-purpose flour
1¹/₂ cups sugar
2 tablespoons baking powder
1 teaspoon salt
³/₄ cup (1¹/₂ sticks) butter, softened
4 eggs
2 cups milk
2 teaspoons vanilla extract
3 cups fresh or frozen blueberries

Mix the flour, sugar, baking powder and salt in a large bowl. Cut in the butter until crumbly. Beat the eggs, milk and vanilla in a bowl. Add to the flour mixture and mix until moistened. Stir in the blueberries gently. Pour into three buttered and floured 4×8-inch loaf pans. Bake at 350 degrees for 1 hour or until the loaves test done. **Makes 3 loaves.**

These loaves freeze well and make great hostess gifts.

Crème Brûlée French Toast

6 tablespoons unsalted butter
1 tablespoon maple syrup
1/2 cup packed brown sugar
1 loaf unsliced egg bread, such as Challah
3/4 cup half-and-half
6 eggs
1 teaspoon vanilla extract
1/4 cup orange juice
1/4 cup granulated sugar
2 teaspoons orange zest
Pinch of salt
Fresh berries (optional)

Melt the butter in a saucepan. Stir in the maple syrup and brown sugar. Cook until the mixture is bubbly. Pour into a 9×9-inch baking dish coated with nonstick cooking spray. Trim the crust from the bread. Cut the bread into 1-inch cubes. Arrange to fit tightly in the syrup mixture. Whisk the half-and-half, eggs, vanilla, orange juice, granulated sugar, orange zest and salt in a bowl. Pour evenly over the bread. Chill, covered with foil, for 2 to 10 hours. Bake, covered, at 350 degrees for 15 minutes. Bake, uncovered, for 30 minutes longer or until puffed and golden brown. Spoon onto serving plates. Sauce from the dish may be spooned alongside the French toast. Top with fresh berries. **Serves 4.**

Two teaspoons Grand Marnier may be substituted for the orange juice.

Jeweled Banana Bread

1³/₄ cups all-purpose flour	1 cup mashed bananas
2³/₄ teaspoons baking powder	(about 3 bananas)
¹/₂ teaspoon salt	¹/₂ cup chopped walnuts
5 tablespoons butter, softened	or pecans
²/₃ cup sugar	1 cup candied fruit cake mix
2 eggs	¹/₄ cup golden raisins

Mix the flour, baking powder and salt together. Cream the butter and sugar in a mixing bowl. Add the eggs and beat until thick. Add the flour mixture and mix well. Fold in the bananas, walnuts, fruit cake mix and raisins. Spoon into a buttered 4×8-inch loaf pan. Bake at 350 degrees for 60 to 70 minutes or until a tester inserted in the center comes out clean. Cool in the pan. **Makes 1 loaf.**

The bread may be baked in three small loaf pans for 45 minutes.
Fruit cake mix is usually found in grocery stores during the holiday
season but is safe to purchase and keep for use throughout the year.

Miniature Parmesan Popovers

3 eggs	¹/₄ cup finely chopped parsley
³/₄ cup all-purpose flour	1 cup milk
¹/₄ to ¹/₂ teaspoon salt	1 cup (4 ounces) finely grated
¹/₂ teaspoon pepper	Parmesan cheese or
¹/₂ teaspoon herbes de Provence	Gruyère cheese

Process the eggs, flour, salt, pepper, herbes de Provence, parsley, milk and Parmesan cheese in a blender until well mixed. Pour into miniature muffin cups sprayed with nonstick baking spray, filling three-fourths full. Bake at 400 degrees for 20 to 25 minutes or until puffed and golden brown. Remove from the pan and serve immediately. **Serves 6 to 8.**

Morning Glory Muffins

2 cups all-purpose flour
1¼ cups sugar
2 teaspoons baking soda
2 teaspoons cinnamon
½ teaspoon salt
1½ cups finely grated carrots
1½ cups finely grated peeled Granny Smith apples
¾ cup finely chopped coconut
½ cup finely chopped dates
½ cup finely chopped pecans
3 eggs, beaten
1 cup vegetable oil
½ teaspoon vanilla extract

Mix the flour, sugar, baking soda, cinnamon and salt in a large bowl. Combine the carrots, apples, coconut, dates and pecans in a bowl and mix well. Stir in the eggs, oil and vanilla. Add to the flour mixture and stir until moistened. Spoon into buttered and floured miniature muffin cups. Bake at 375 degrees for 11 to 15 minutes or until a tester inserted near the center comes out clean. **Makes 40 to 48 miniature muffins.**

*Golden raisins, bananas, or cranberries may be used. The batter
may be baked in large muffin cups for 20 to 25 minutes.*

Orange Rolls

1/4 **cup sugar, divided**
1 **tablespoon fresh orange juice**
2 **teaspoons (heaping) orange zest, divided**
1 **(8-count) can refrigerator crescent rolls**
1/8 **teaspoon cinnamon (optional)**
4 **teaspoons butter, melted**

Combine 2 tablespoons of the sugar, the orange juice and 1 heaping teaspoon of the orange zest in a bowl and mix well. Set the topping aside. Unroll the crescent roll dough. Separate the dough into two rectangles, pressing the perforations to seal.

Combine the remaining 2 tablespoons sugar, remaining 1 heaping teaspoon orange zest and the cinnamon in a small bowl. Brush each rectangle with the butter. Sprinkle with the sugar mixture. Roll up each rectangle to enclose the filling, beginning with the short end. Freeze the roll-ups for 10 to 15 minutes.

Remove from the freezer and cut into eight rolls. Place cut side down in a generously buttered 8-inch round baking pan. Top each roll with 2 teaspoons of the topping. Bake at 375 degrees for 18 to 22 minutes or until golden brown. Invert onto a serving plate and immediately invert each roll so that the topping is on top. Delicious served warm. **Makes 8 rolls.**

*To easily remove the rolls from the pan, generously
butter the entire baking pan.*

Prosciutto Breakfast Rolls

2 (8-count) cans refrigerator crescent rolls
16 thin slices prosciutto
2 tablespoons honey
2 tablespoons Dijon mustard

Unroll the crescent roll dough. Separate the dough into eight rectangles, pressing the perforations to seal. Top each rectangle with two slices prosciutto. Roll up to enclose the filling, beginning at the long side. Cut each roll-up crosswise into halves. Place seam side down on a baking sheet coated with nonstick cooking spray. Whisk the honey and Dijon mustard in a bowl. Brush over the tops of the rolls. Bake at 375 degrees for 12 minutes or until golden brown. **Makes 16 rolls.**

Rich Raisin Bread

5 to 5$^{1}/_{2}$ cups all-purpose flour, divided
2 envelopes dry yeast
$^{1}/_{2}$ cup sugar
1 teaspoon salt
$^{3}/_{4}$ cup milk
$^{1}/_{2}$ cup water
$^{1}/_{2}$ cup (1 stick) butter
2 eggs
1$^{1}/_{2}$ cups raisins

Combine 2$^{1}/_{2}$ cups of the flour, the yeast, sugar and salt in a large mixing bowl and mix well. Heat the milk, water and butter in a saucepan just until warm. Add to the flour mixture. Stir in the eggs. Beat at low speed until moistened. Beat at medium speed for 3 minutes. Stir in the raisins and enough of the remaining flour gradually by hand to make a firm dough. Knead the dough on a floured surface for 5 to 8 minutes or until smooth and elastic. Place in a greased bowl, turning to coat the surface. Cover and let rise in a warm place for 1 hour or until doubled in bulk.

Punch down the dough. Divide the dough into two equal portions. Roll or pat each portion into a 7×14-inch rectangle on a lightly floured surface. Roll each up tightly beginning with the short side and pressing the dough into the roll with each turn. Pinch the edges and ends to seal. Place in two buttered 4×8-inch loaf pans or 5×9-inch loaf pans. Cover and let rise for 45 to 60 minutes or until doubled in bulk. Bake at 350 degrees for 40 to 45 minutes or until golden brown, covering loosely with foil if the loaves begin to overbrown. Invert onto a wire rack to cool completely. **Makes 2 loaves.**

Simply delicious when toasted.

Tipsy Peach Bread

1 (16-ounce) package frozen sliced peaches, thawed
1/2 cup dark rum
1 3/4 cups all-purpose flour
1 cup sugar
1 teaspoon baking powder
1 teaspoon baking soda
1/2 teaspoon salt
1/2 teaspoon cinnamon
1/4 teaspoon ground allspice
1/8 teaspoon ground cloves
1 egg, beaten
3 tablespoons butter, melted
1 teaspoon vanilla extract
3/4 cup chopped almonds

Cook the peaches and rum in a saucepan over medium heat for 15 minutes, stirring frequently. Process in a blender until smooth. Mix the flour, sugar, baking powder, baking soda, salt, cinnamon, allspice and cloves in a large bowl. Stir in the peach mixture, egg, butter and vanilla. Stir in the almonds. Spoon into a buttered and floured 4×8-inch loaf pan. Bake at 350 degrees for 30 minutes; cover with foil to prevent overbrowning. Bake for 15 minutes longer or until the bread tests done. Cool in the pan for 10 to 15 minutes. Invert onto a wire rack to cool completely. **Makes 1 loaf.**

Soups
& Salads

Dating back to 1857, the seaside community of Fernandina Beach and its historic downtown buildings remain as some of the best examples of Victorian-era architecture on the eastern seacoast. Shops and restaurants line Centre Street as it stretches from the harbor to the Atlantic Ocean. The Palace Saloon began serving folks in 1903 and is the oldest continuously operating saloon in Florida.

PALACE
PALACE SALOON
PARKING
ONE WAY
Intercoastal Wine Co.
Trailer Park Collectibles
Wicked Davey's Fancy Saloon
THREE BLOCKS NORTH
ART GALLERY
Pablo's
The Crab Trap
Restaurant & Tavern
FLORIDA YACHT
PABLO'S MEXICAN RESTAURANT

Gumbo

6 to 8 slices bacon
Vegetable oil
3/4 cup all-purpose flour
5 (10-ounce) cans chicken broth
3 (14-ounce) cans tomatoes
1 (8-ounce) can tomato sauce
2 (10-ounce) packages frozen chopped okra
2 onions, chopped
2 green bell peppers, chopped
8 ribs celery, chopped
4 carrots, chopped
10 green onions, chopped
5 garlic cloves, minced
1/2 cup vegetable oil
8 boneless skinless chicken breasts, cooked and chopped
8 hot Italian sausage links, cooked and chopped

2 thick ham slices, cooked and chopped
1 tablespoon marjoram
1 tablespoon Tabasco sauce
1 tablespoon red pepper flakes
1 tablespoon Worcestershire sauce
4 bay leaves
2 teaspoons salt
2 teaspoons black pepper
2 tablespoons parsley
1/2 teaspoon thyme
1/2 teaspoon oregano
2 pounds shrimp, cooked, peeled and deveined
Filé powder to taste
Hot cooked rice

Cook the bacon in a Dutch oven until crisp. Remove the bacon to paper towels to drain. Add enough oil to the bacon drippings to measure 3/4 cup. Stir in the flour to form a roux. Cook over low heat until the roux is brown, stirring constantly. Add the broth gradually, stirring constantly. Add the tomatoes, tomato sauce and okra.

Sauté the onions, bell peppers, celery, carrots, green onions and garlic in 1/2 cup oil in a large skillet until tender. Add to the tomato mixture. Stir in the chicken, sausage, ham and bacon. Add the marjoram, Tabasco sauce, red pepper flakes, Worcestershire sauce, bay leaves, salt, black pepper, parsley, thyme and oregano and mix well. Simmer for 2 hours or longer. Stir in the shrimp. Cook until heated through. Discard the bay leaves. Stir in filé powder just before serving. Serve over rice. **Serves 18 to 20.**

The Real McCoy! This recipe freezes well and improves with each reheating. Add additional broth if the gumbo is too thick. Filé powder can be found in the spice section of your grocery store.

Meatball Soup

1 (15-ounce) can beef broth
1 (14-ounce) can crushed tomatoes
1 envelope dry onion soup mix
1/2 cup chopped celery
1/4 cup chopped parsley
1 teaspoon oregano, divided
1 bay leaf
2 cups water
2 cups sliced carrots
1 1/2 pounds ground beef
1 egg
1/2 cup milk
1/2 cup dry bread crumbs
1 teaspoon salt
Grated Parmesan cheese to taste

Combine the broth, tomatoes, onion soup mix, celery, parsley, 1/2 teaspoon of the oregano, the bay leaf and water in a large stockpot. Bring to a boil; reduce the heat. Simmer for 50 minutes. Add the carrots and simmer for 10 minutes longer.

Combine the ground beef, egg, milk, bread crumbs, salt and the remaining 1/2 teaspoon oregano in a bowl and mix well. Shape into miniature meatballs and place on a rimmed baking sheet. Bake at 350 degrees for 15 minutes. Add to the soup. Cook for 20 minutes. Discard the bay leaf. Ladle into soup bowls and sprinkle with Parmesan cheese. **Serves 6 to 8.**

*A unique soup presentation. Browned ground beef
can be used instead of meatballs.*

Minestrone alla Novarese

1/3 cup olive oil
2 tablespoons butter
2 cups thinly sliced onions
8 ounces Canadian bacon, chopped
4 ribs celery, chopped
3 large carrots, chopped
4 zucchini, chopped
2 cups shredded red cabbage or Savoy cabbage
1 cup (or more) undrained canned chopped Italian tomatoes
Salt and pepper to taste
4 cups chicken broth
2 cups drained cannellini beans
Freshly grated Parmesan cheese to taste

Heat the olive oil and butter in a large stockpot. Add the onions and bacon and sauté until brown. Add the celery, carrots, zucchini and cabbage one at a time in the order listed, stirring and cooking for 3 minutes after each addition. Add the tomatoes, salt and pepper. Stir in the broth. The vegetables should be covered by 1 inch of liquid. If not, add additional undrained tomatoes. Cover and bring to a boil. Reduce the heat. Barely simmer for 1 3/4 hours over low heat. Add the beans. Simmer for 15 minutes longer or until the soup is thick. Adjust the seasonings to taste. Ladle into soup bowls and sprinkle with Parmesan cheese. **Serves 4 to 6.**

*This hearty version of minestrone is great on its own
and improves if made in advance and reheated. Small quantities
of leftovers may be expanded by adding additional
broth and cooked pasta or rice.*

Pumpkin and Squash Soup

3 tablespoons unsalted butter, divided	1 tablespoon brown sugar
1 tablespoon olive oil	2 teaspoons kosher salt
2 cups chopped onions	1/2 teaspoon pepper
1 (15-ounce) can pumpkin purée	1 cup half-and-half
1 1/2 pounds butternut squash, peeled and cut into chunks	2 slices white bread, cut into 1/2-inch cubes
4 cups chicken broth	Salt and pepper to taste
Pinch of mace	Shredded Gruyère cheese to taste

Heat 2 tablespoons of the butter and the olive oil in a stockpot. Add the onions. Cook over medium-low heat for 10 minutes or until translucent. Add the pumpkin, squash, broth, mace, brown sugar, kosher salt and 1/2 teaspoon pepper. Simmer, covered, over medium-low heat for 20 minutes or until the squash is very tender. Process in a food processor until blended. Return to the stockpot. Stir in the half-and-half. Heat over low heat until heated through. Adjust the kosher salt to taste. Sauté the bread in the remaining 1 tablespoon butter in a skillet until brown. Sprinkle with salt and pepper to taste. Ladle the soup into serving bowls. Top with the croutons and sprinkle with Gruyère cheese. **Serves 6 to 8.**

Roasted Carrot and Parsnip Soup

1 pound carrots, peeled and chopped	3 tablespoons olive oil
8 ounces parsnips, peeled and chopped	1 teaspoon salt
	1/4 teaspoon pepper
1 onion, cut into quarters	8 cups (about) chicken broth

Place the carrots, parsnips and onion on a rimmed baking sheet. Add the olive oil and toss to coat. Sprinkle with the salt and pepper. Roast at 400 degrees for 45 to 60 minutes or until very tender. Remove the vegetables to a bowl. Add enough broth to the drippings in the rimmed baking sheet to aid in scraping up any brown bits. Purée the vegetables in batches in a food processor, adding enough of the broth to dilute to the desired consistency. Place in a large stockpot. Heat the soup and then ladle into soup bowls. **Serves 4 to 6.**

Milk, cream, or water may be used instead of the broth to dilute the soup to the desired consistency.

Sausage Tortellini Soup

1 pound sweet Italian sausage,
      casings removed
1 large onion, chopped
1 garlic clove, minced
3 (14-ounce) cans beef broth
2 (14-ounce) cans diced tomatoes
1 (8-ounce) can tomato sauce
1 cup dry red wine

2 carrots, thinly sliced
1 tablespoon sugar
2 teaspoons Italian seasoning
2 small zucchini, sliced
9 ounces refrigerator
      cheese tortellini
1/2 cup (2 ounces) grated
      Parmesan cheese

Brown the Italian sausage, onion and garlic in a Dutch oven over medium heat, stirring until the Italian sausage is crumbly; drain. Stir in the broth, undrained tomatoes, tomato sauce, wine, carrots, sugar and Italian seasoning. Bring to a boil; reduce the heat. Simmer for 30 minutes. Skim the surface. Stir in the zucchini and tortellini. Simmer for 10 minutes. Ladle into soup bowls and sprinkle with the Parmesan cheese. **Serves 6 to 8.**

This soup freezes well.

Shrimp and Vegetable Soup

2 tablespoons butter
1 cup finely chopped parsnips
2 leeks, finely chopped
4 ribs celery, finely chopped
4 bay leaves
1 cup white wine
32 medium shrimp, peeled
      and deveined

2 cups heavy cream
Salt and pepper to taste
2 tomatoes, peeled and chopped
      for garnish
3 tablespoons chopped chives for
      garnish

Melt the butter in a large saucepan. Add the parsnips, leeks, celery and bay leaves and sauté for 2 minutes. Add the wine. Cook until the liquid is reduced by one-half. Add the shrimp. Cook for 1 minute. Add the cream. Simmer for 3 to 4 minutes. Add salt and pepper. Discard the bay leaves. Ladle into soup bowls. Garnish with the tomatoes and chives. **Serves 4 to 6.**

A rich soup.

Southwestern Chicken and Rice Soup

1 onion, chopped	1 teaspoon ground cumin
1 large carrot, peeled and chopped	1/4 teaspoon pepper
1/2 red bell pepper, chopped	8 cups chicken broth
1 tablespoon vegetable oil	2 cups shredded cooked chicken
2 garlic cloves, minced	1/4 cup chopped cilantro leaves
3/4 cup uncooked white rice	2 tablespoons lime juice
2 plum tomatoes, chopped	1 avocado, chopped for garnish
1 to 2 tablespoons chopped pickled jalapeño chile slices	1 (3-ounce) package tri-colored tortilla strips for garnish

Sauté the onion, carrot and bell pepper in the oil in a Dutch oven over medium heat for 7 minutes or until the vegetables are tender. Add the garlic and sauté for 1 minute. Stir in the rice, tomatoes, jalapeño chiles, cumin and pepper. Add the broth. Bring to a boil; reduce the heat. Simmer for 20 minutes or until the rice is tender. Stir in the chicken, cilantro and lime juice. Cook until heated through. Ladle into soup bowls. Garnish with the avocado and tortilla strips. **Serves 6 to 8.**

Brown rice may be used instead of the white rice.
Prepare the recipe as directed, but increase the simmering time
to 45 minutes or until the rice is tender.

White Summer Soup

3 English cucumbers	2 teaspoons salt
3 cups chicken broth, divided	2 tomatoes, peeled and chopped
3 cups sour cream	1/2 cup thinly sliced green onions
3 tablespoons white vinegar	1/2 cup chopped parsley
1 tablespoon white wine	1/2 cup chopped almonds, toasted
1 garlic clove, crushed	

Peel and coarsely chop the cucumbers. Process the cucumbers with 1 1/2 cups of the broth in a blender for 1 minute. Combine the remaining 1 1/2 cups broth, the sour cream, vinegar, wine, garlic and salt in a large bowl. Whisk in the cucumber purée. Chill until serving time. Ladle into soup bowls or mugs. Sprinkle with the tomatoes, green onions, parsley and almonds. **Serves 6 to 8.**

Bok Choy Salad

1 cup canola oil	1 tablespoon butter
³/4 cup sugar	1 tablespoon olive oil
2 teaspoons soy sauce	1 (2-ounce) package
¹/2 cup rice wine vinegar	slivered almonds
1 (3-ounce) package oriental	1 head bok choy
Ramen noodles	4 green onions, chopped

Whisk the canola oil, sugar, soy sauce and vinegar in a bowl until blended. Crush the Ramen noodles in a plastic bag, reserving the flavor packet. Melt the butter and olive oil in a small skillet. Add the Ramen noodles and almonds. Sauté until light brown. Stir in the seasonings from the reserved packet. Let stand until cool. Julienne the white and green portions of the bok choy. Combine with the green onions in a large bowl. Add one-half of the dressing and mix well. Add additional dressing if needed. Add the noodle mixture and toss well. Serve immediately. **Serves 6 to 8.**

This is a great complement to pork. The leftovers are good the next day even when the noodles are soft. Substitute broccoli slaw for the bok choy and add 1 cup raisins for variation.

Chickpea Salad

3 tablespoons olive oil	¹/2 cup black olives, pitted
2 tablespoons white wine vinegar	and chopped
¹/2 teaspoon salt	3 plum tomatoes, seeded
¹/2 teaspoon pepper	and chopped
2 (15-ounce) cans chickpeas,	3 green onions, chopped
drained and rinsed	¹/4 cup chopped fresh parsley
1 small cucumber, peeled, seeded	Chopped romaine
and chopped	

Whisk the olive oil, vinegar, salt and pepper in a bowl. Combine the chickpeas, cucumber, olives, tomatoes, green onions and parsley in a bowl. Add the vinaigrette and toss to mix. Serve over a small bed of romaine on individual salad plates. **Serves 6.**

Coconut Curried Rice Salad

1¹/3 cups rice	1 teaspoon salt
¹/2 cup chicken broth	1 cup chopped celery
¹/2 cup water	¹/3 cup chopped red or green
¹/4 cup chopped onion	bell pepper
1¹/2 tablespoons white vinegar	¹/3 cup raisins
2 tablespoons vegetable oil	¹/3 cup shredded coconut
1¹/2 teaspoons curry powder, or	¹/3 cup chutney
to taste	³/4 cup mayonnaise
¹/2 teaspoon ginger	

Cook the rice using the package directions, omitting the butter and using the broth and water for the liquid. Remove from the heat. Combine the rice, onion, vinegar, oil, curry powder, ginger and salt in a bowl and toss lightly. Chill, covered, for 3 hours. Stir in the celery, bell pepper, raisins, coconut, chutney and mayonnaise just before serving. **Serves 6.**

Cooked chicken or shrimp may be added to make this an entrée.
For a nice crunch, add ¹/3 cup chopped peanuts.

Cranberry Coleslaw

5 cups shredded cabbage	1 cup julienned jicama (optional)
¹/2 cup toasted almonds	¹/2 cup mayonnaise
1¹/2 cups dried cranberries	1 tablespoon sweet pickle relish
¹/2 cup chopped celery	1 tablespoon honey mustard
¹/4 cup chopped green onions	1 tablespoon honey
(white and green portions)	Salt and pepper to taste
¹/2 cup chopped green bell pepper	

Combine the cabbage, almonds, cranberries, celery, green onions, bell pepper and jicama in a large bowl and mix well. Chill, covered, until serving time. Combine the mayonnaise, pickle relish, honey mustard and honey in a bowl and mix well. Season with salt and pepper. Chill, covered, until serving time. To serve, add the dressing to the cabbage mixture and toss to coat. **Serves 10 to 12.**

The jicama adds more crunch to the coleslaw.

Cucumber Salad

1/2 cup thinly sliced red onion	2 tablespoons minced fresh mint
4 cucumbers	1/4 cup minced parsley
1 teaspoon salt	2 green onions, sliced
Pepper to taste	1 to 2 tablespoons minced fresh
3/4 cup sour cream or yogurt	dill weed
1 or 2 garlic cloves, minced	1 cup chopped walnuts, lightly
1 to 2 teaspoons honey	toasted
1 1/2 teaspoons tarragon vinegar	

Soak the onion in cold water for 30 minutes. Drain the onion well and pat dry. Peel the cucumbers and remove the seeds. Cut the cucumbers into thin slices and place in a medium bowl. Add the onion, salt, pepper, sour cream, garlic, honey, vinegar, mint, parsley, green onions and dill weed and mix well. Chill, covered, until serving time. Sprinkle with the walnuts before serving. **Serves 6.**

Edamame Salad

1 (15-ounce) can black beans, drained and rinsed (optional)	1/4 cup apricot preserves
1 pound green beans	1 tablespoon sugar
1 (10-ounce) package shelled edamame	1 teaspoon grated fresh ginger
3 tablespoons canola oil	Red leaf lettuce
2 tablespoons rice wine vinegar	2 green onions, chopped, for garnish

Combine the black beans, green beans and edamame in a bowl. Whisk the oil, vinegar, apricot preserves, sugar and ginger in a bowl. Pour over the beans and toss to coat. Serve on red leaf lettuce-lined salad plates. Garnish with the green onions. **Serves 4 to 6.**

Far East Spinach Salad

1/4 cup white wine vinegar
1/4 cup vegetable oil
2 tablespoons chutney
2 teaspoons sugar
1/4 teaspoon salt
1 1/2 teaspoons curry powder
1 teaspoon dry mustard

1 (5-ounce) package
  baby spinach
1 1/2 cups chopped unpeeled
  Golden Delicious apples
1/2 cup raisins
1/2 cup peanuts, chopped
2 tablespoons sliced green onions

Combine the vinegar, oil, chutney, sugar, salt, curry powder and dry mustard in a jar with a tight-fitting lid. Chill, covered, until serving time. Place the spinach in a salad bowl. Top with the apples, raisins, peanuts and green onions. Shake the dressing. Pour over the salad and toss to coat. **Serves 4.**

Fig and Stilton Salad

3/4 cup ruby Port
1/4 cup dry red wine
1/4 cup vegetable oil
3 tablespoons balsamic vinegar
2 tablespoons walnut oil
1 tablespoon sugar
1 tablespoon red wine vinegar
1 1/2 teaspoons Worcestershire
  sauce

1 1/2 teaspoons light molasses
1/4 teaspoon onion powder
1 (9-ounce) package dried black
  Mission figs
Salt and pepper to taste
1 (5-ounce) package mixed baby
  salad greens
4 ounces Stilton cheese, crumbled

Whisk the Port, red wine, vegetable oil, balsamic vinegar, walnut oil, sugar, red wine vinegar, Worcestershire sauce, molasses and onion powder in a bowl. Chill, covered, for up to 3 days. Remove the stems from the figs. Cut the figs lengthwise into halves. Bring the figs and the vinaigrette to simmer in a skillet over medium heat. Cook for 8 minutes or until the mixture resembles a thin syrup. Cool slightly. Sprinkle with salt and pepper. Divide the salad greens among six salad plates and sprinkle with the cheese. Ladle the warm fig dressing over the top and serve immediately. **Serves 6.**

If black Mission figs are not available, use one
14-ounce package of dried figs.

Hearts of Palm and Artichoke Salad

Creamy Herb Dressing
6 tablespoons vegetable oil
6 tablespoons tarragon vinegar
1/2 teaspoon pepper
1/4 teaspoon garlic salt
2 teaspoons Dijon mustard
1/2 cup mayonnaise
1/4 teaspoon dill weed
1 teaspoon sugar

Salad
2 cups torn romaine
1 cup torn iceberg lettuce
1 cup torn Bibb lettuce
1 (14-ounce) can hearts of palm, drained and sliced
1 (14-ounce) can artichoke hearts, drained and quartered
1/2 cup grated carrots
2 tablespoons chopped parsley
2 tomatoes, chopped

To prepare the dressing, combine the oil, vinegar, pepper, garlic salt, Dijon mustard, mayonnaise, dill weed and sugar in a bowl and mix well. Chill, covered, until serving time.

To prepare the salad, mix the romaine, iceberg lettuce and Bibb lettuce in a large bowl. Add the hearts of palm, artichoke hearts, carrots, parsley and tomatoes. Chill, covered, until serving time.

To serve, pour the dressing over the salad and toss to coat. **Serves 8 to 10.**

Oriental Chicken Salad

2/3 cup mayonnaise
1/4 teaspoon sesame oil
1/2 teaspoon soy sauce
1 green onion, chopped
2 ribs celery, chopped
2 cups chopped cooked chicken
2 cups red seedless grapes, cut into halves
Salt and pepper to taste
Chopped romaine
Chopped cashews for garnish

Blend the mayonnaise, sesame oil and soy sauce in a bowl. Combine the green onion, celery, chicken and grapes in a bowl and mix well. Add the mayonnaise mixture and toss to coat. Sprinkle with salt and pepper. Serve over a bed of chopped romaine on salad plates. Garnish with chopped cashews. **Serves 4.**

Roasted Beet, Pistachio and Pear Salad

2 fresh beets (about 12 ounces)
1 cup chopped ripe pear
1/4 cup chopped celery
2 tablespoons chopped pistachios
3 tablespoons fresh lemon juice
1 tablespoon honey
1/2 teaspoon brown sugar
Salt to taste
1/4 teaspoon black pepper
Dash of ground red pepper
2 leaves curly leaf lettuce
  (optional)

Leave the root and 1 inch of the stem on each beet. Scrub with a brush. Wrap in foil. Bake at 350 degrees for 1 to 1 1/2 hours. Chill in the refrigerator. Peel and chop the beets. Combine the beets, pear, celery and pistachios in a medium bowl. Whisk the lemon juice, honey, brown sugar, salt, black pepper and red pepper in a bowl. Drizzle over the beet mixture and toss gently to coat. Serve chilled on the lettuce leaves or at room temperature. **Serves 2.**

Sauerkraut Salad

1 (27-ounce) jar
  sauerkraut, drained
1 large green bell pepper, chopped
1 cup chopped celery
1 onion, chopped
1 (2-ounce) jar pimento, chopped
1 cup shredded carrots (optional)
1/2 cup apple cider vinegar
1/4 cup water
1 teaspoon salt
1/4 teaspoon pepper
1 to 1 1/2 cups sugar
Lettuce leaves
Chopped parsley

Combine the sauerkraut, bell pepper, celery, onion, pimento and carrots in a large bowl and mix well. Whisk the vinegar, water, salt, pepper and sugar in a small bowl until the sugar dissolves. Pour over the sauerkraut mixture and mix well. Chill, covered, for 30 minutes or longer before serving. Spoon into a lettuce-lined salad bowl and sprinkle with parsley. **Serves 6 to 8.**

Spaghetti Squash Salad

4 cups spaghetti squash (about 2 pounds)
1 (6-ounce) jar marinated artichoke hearts
1 zucchini, cut into thin strips
1 carrot, peeled and cut into thin strips
2/3 cup chopped red bell pepper
1 cup (4 ounces) shredded mozzarella cheese
2 tablespoons grated Parmesan cheese
1/4 cup rice wine vinegar
1 tablespoon dry mustard
1 tablespoon chopped fresh oregano
1 tablespoon chopped fresh basil
1 tablespoon chopped fresh parsley
1 tablespoon finely chopped onion
2 tablespoons capers, crushed
2 tablespoons vegetable oil
2 tablespoons red wine vinegar
1 teaspoon dry white wine (optional)
1 garlic clove, minced
Lawry's seasoned salt to taste
Pepper to taste

Pierce the squash generously with a knife. Microwave on High for 15 minutes or until tender when pierced with a skewer. Cool for 10 minutes. Cut the squash into halves and remove the seeds. Scrape the strands into a large bowl and separate with a fork to resemble spaghetti. Drain the artichokes, reserving the marinade. Chop the artichokes coarsely. Add the artichokes, zucchini, carrot, bell pepper, mozzarella cheese and Parmesan cheese to the squash and mix well. Combine the reserved marinade, the rice vinegar, dry mustard, oregano, basil, parsley, onion, capers, oil, red wine vinegar, wine and garlic in a jar with a tight-fitting lid. Cover the jar and shake vigorously. Season with Lawry's salt and the pepper. Pour over the vegetable mixture. Chill, covered, for 8 hours. **Serves 8 to 10.**

Succotash Salad

1/2 to 1 cup bow tie pasta
1 (8-ounce) package French-style green beans
1 (10-ounce) package frozen baby lima beans
1 (11-ounce) can niblets corn, drained
1 cup (4 ounces) grated asiago cheese or Parmesan cheese
6 green onions, chopped
3 plum tomatoes, seeded and chopped
Newman's Own Caesar dressing to taste
Salt and pepper to taste
8 ounces bacon, crisp-cooked and crumbled

Cook the pasta, green beans and lima beans separately using the package directions; drain and cool. Combine the pasta, cooked vegetables, corn, cheese, green onions and tomatoes in a bowl. Add dressing and toss to coat. Sprinkle with salt and pepper. Stir in the bacon just before serving. Serve at room temperature. **Serves 6 to 8.**

Julienned spinach or romaine may be substituted
for the pasta. One pound of chopped blanched asparagus may
be used for either of the green vegetables.

Turkey Orzo Salad

8 ounces tri-colored orzo

4 cups bite-size pieces roasted turkey breast

1 red bell pepper, finely chopped

1 yellow bell pepper, finely chopped

1 (15-ounce) can black beans, drained and rinsed

1/2 cup thinly sliced green onions

1 cup corn kernels

1 large tomato, seeded and chopped

1/3 cup finely chopped cilantro

3 tablespoons fresh lime juice

1 1/2 tablespoons white wine vinegar

2 garlic cloves, minced

1/2 teaspoon salt

1/2 teaspoon pepper

1 or 2 jalapeño chiles, seeded and chopped

1 1/2 teaspoons ground cumin

2/3 cup olive oil

Romaine leaves

2 avocados, chopped for garnish

Cook the pasta using the package directions. Combine the pasta, turkey, bell peppers, beans, green onions, corn, tomato and cilantro in a large bowl and mix well. Combine the lime juice, vinegar, garlic, 1/2 teaspoon salt, 1/2 teaspoon pepper, the jalapeño chiles and cumin in a food processor. Add the olive oil in a steady stream, processing constantly to emulsify. Pour over the turkey mixture and toss to coat. Adjust seasoning if needed. Spoon into a romaine-lined salad bowl and garnish with the avocado. **Serves 6 to 8.**

Vegetable Salad

1 cup chopped blanched asparagus
1 cup chopped cucumber
1 cup chopped sugar snap peas
1/4 cup chopped roasted red pepper
1/4 cup chopped cooked bacon
1/4 cup crumbled blue cheese
1/4 cup olive oil
2 tablespoons balsamic vinegar
Salt and pepper to taste
1 avocado, sliced for garnish

Combine the asparagus, cucumber, peas, red pepper, bacon and cheese in a bowl and mix well. Whisk the olive oil, balsamic vinegar, salt and pepper in a bowl. Pour over the vegetables. Divide the salad among four to six chilled salad plates. Garnish with the avocado. **Serves 4 to 6.**

This salad looks great mounded in the center of the plate and surrounded by mixed salad greens. Delicious with chicken or shrimp added for a luncheon or light supper.

Fabulous Dressing

1 cup vegetable oil
1/2 cup sugar
1/3 cup ketchup
1/2 cup cider vinegar
1 tablespoon Worcestershire sauce
1 onion, chopped
1 teaspoon salt

Process the oil, sugar, ketchup, vinegar, Worcestershire sauce, onion and salt in a blender until blended. Serve with spinach or any type of salad greens. **Makes about 3 cups.**

Meats
& Poultry

In our historic downtown, the Fernandina Beach Post Office, circa 1912,
was the first all-steel structure on Amelia Island. It is an architectural replica of
the de Medici Palazzo in Florence, Italy. Designed in the Italian
Renaissance Revival style, the post office continues to process mail and to
enchant visitors and residents alike in today's twenty-first century.

Beef Fillets with Stilton Portobello Sauce

6 (6-ounce) beef tenderloin fillets
2 teaspoons chopped fresh tarragon
1/2 teaspoon freshly ground pepper
5 tablespoons butter, divided
8 ounces portobello mushroom caps, sliced
1/2 cup dry red wine or beef broth
1/2 cup sour cream
3 ounces Stilton cheese or other blue cheese, crumbled and divided
6 sprigs of fresh tarragon, finely chopped for garnish

Rub the fillets with 2 teaspoons tarragon and the pepper. Melt 2 tablespoons of the butter in a large skillet over medium-high heat. Add the fillets. Cook for 4 to 5 minutes on each side or to the desired degree of doneness. Keep warm.

Sauté the mushrooms in the remaining 3 tablespoons butter for 3 to 4 minutes or until tender. Add the wine. Cook for 1 to 2 minutes. Stir in the sour cream. Add 1/4 cup of the cheese. Cook until the cheese melts, stirring constantly. Spoon over the fillets. Sprinkle with the remaining cheese. Garnish with the chopped tarragon sprigs. **Serves 6.**

The beef may also be grilled.

Flank Steak Marinades

Spicy Marinade
1 cup ketchup
3 tablespoons apple cider vinegar
2 tablespoons vegetable oil
2 tablespoons steak sauce
1 tablespoon spicy brown mustard
Hot pepper sauce to taste
Kosher salt to taste
Pepper to taste

Asian Marinade
1/2 cup soy sauce
1 garlic clove, minced
2 tablespoons Worcestershire sauce
2 tablespoons lemon juice
2 tablespoons vegetable oil
1 tablespoon dried minced onion
1 teaspoon ginger
1/4 teaspoon pepper
1 teaspoon parsley

Steak
1 (2-pound) flank steak

To prepare the spicy marinade, mix the ketchup, vinegar, oil, steak sauce, mustard, pepper sauce, kosher salt and pepper in a bowl.

To prepare the Asian marinade, combine the soy sauce, garlic, Worcestershire sauce, lemon juice, oil, onion, ginger, pepper and parsley in a bowl and mix well.

To prepare the steak, place the steak in a sealable plastic bag. Pour either the spicy marinade or the Asian marinade over the steak and seal the bag. Marinate in the refrigerator for 2 to 4 hours. Drain the steak, discarding the marinade. Place the steak on a grill rack. Grill over medium-high heat for 5 minutes. Turn and grill for 4 minutes longer. Let stand for 5 minutes. Cut the steak diagonally into slices and serve. **Serves 6.**

Florentine Stuffed Meat Loaf

1 pound ground bulk Italian sausage
1 pound ground chuck
1 pound ground veal
1 onion, chopped
2 cups dry bread crumbs
2 eggs, beaten
1/2 cup tomato sauce
1/2 cup red wine
1 tablespoon oregano
1 teaspoon salt
1 teaspoon pepper
1 pound baby bello mushrooms (Crimini)
2 tablespoons butter
1/4 cup Marsala wine
1 cup fresh spinach, rinsed and patted dry
16 ounces mozzarella cheese, thinly sliced
Marinara sauce, heated

Combine the sausage, ground chuck, ground veal, onion, bread crumbs, eggs, tomato sauce, red wine, oregano, salt and pepper in a bowl and mix well. Sauté the mushrooms in the butter and Marsala wine in a skillet until soft. Place the meat mixture in a foil-lined 10×15-inch baking pan and shape into a rectangle. Layer the spinach, sautéed mushrooms and cheese down the center of the rectangle. Bring the meat sides over the layers and press the seams together to enclose the layers. Bake at 350 degrees for 1 hour. Top with your favorite marinara sauce and serve. **Serves 8.**

German Pot Roast

4 pounds chuck roast or shoulder roast
Salt and pepper to taste
2 onions, sliced
1 (10-ounce) can beef broth
1/3 cup packed brown sugar
1/3 cup cider vinegar
8 gingersnaps, crumbled
8 ounces egg noodles, cooked

Sprinkle the beef with salt and pepper. Place in a slow cooker. Add the onions, broth, brown sugar and vinegar. Cook, tightly covered, on High for 5 to 6 hours, turning occasionally. Remove the beef to a plate. Cut into slices and keep warm. Add the gingersnaps to the sauce in the slow cooker. Cook until thickened, stirring constantly. Place the noodles on a serving platter. Layer the beef and some of the sauce over the noodles. Serve the remaining sauce on the side. **Serves 8.**

Delicious for family or company.

Individual Beef Wellingtons

Beef Wellingtons
8 beef fillets, 1¹/4 to 1¹/2 inches thick
Lawry's seasoned salt to taste
Pepper to taste
Butter for searing
2 (8-count) cans refrigerator crescent rolls
1 pound pork sausage, cut into 16 (¹/4-inch-thick) slices
1 pound mushrooms, sliced
¹/2 cup (1 stick) butter, cut into 16 pieces

Horseradish Sauce
¹/4 cup horseradish
¹/2 teaspoon salt
1 cup sour cream

To prepare the beef Wellingtons, sprinkle the fillets with the seasoned salt and pepper. Brown in butter in a large skillet coated with nonstick cooking spray until the sides and edges are seared. Remove to paper towels to drain. Unroll the crescent roll dough. Press the seams of two of the triangles together on floured waxed paper. Roll into a 7-inch square. Layer 1 slice of the sausage, 4 or 5 mushroom slices, 1 pat of the butter, 1 fillet, 4 or 5 mushroom slices, 1 pat of the butter and 1 slice of the sausage in the order listed in the center of the square. Wrap the dough over the layers, beginning with the opposite corners until completely enclosed. Repeat with the remaining ingredients.

Place the beef Wellingtons seam side down in a large baking pan. Cut an "X" in the top of each and chill in the refrigerator. Remove from the refrigerator and let stand for 30 minutes. Bake at 475 degrees for 10 to 12 minutes or until the crust looks light brown and a knife inserted into the center of the fillet feels warm to the touch.

To prepare the sauce, mix the horseradish, salt and sour cream in a bowl. Chill in the refrigerator. Remove from the refrigerator 30 minutes before serving to bring to room temperature. Serve with the beef Wellingtons. **Serves 8.**

Mrs. Filbert's Best Barbecue Beef

4 **pounds sirloin tip or rump roast, cut into chunks**
2 **tablespoons olive oil**
1/2 **cup red wine**
8 **ribs celery, chopped**
4 **onions, chopped**
1 **(14-ounce) bottle ketchup**
2 **tablespoons vinegar**
1/4 **cup plus 1 tablespoon packed brown sugar**
1 **teaspoon dry mustard**
1 **teaspoon Worcestershire sauce**
Salt and pepper to taste
Crusty rolls, split

Brown the beef in the olive oil in a large ovenproof pan. Add the wine, celery and onions.
Bake, covered, at 300 degrees for 4 to 5 hours or until the beef is very tender. Remove
the beef from the pan to cool. Shred the beef. Strain the vegetables from the broth, reserving
1 1/2 cups of the broth for the sauce. Combine the beef and vegetables in a large bowl.
Combine the reserved broth, the ketchup, vinegar, brown sugar, dry mustard and
Worcestershire sauce in a saucepan and mix well. Bring to a boil and boil for 10 minutes.
Add to the beef mixture with salt and pepper and mix well. Serve on crusty rolls.
Serves 10 to 15.

Great for a crowd and even better served the next day.

Gyro Lamb Burgers with Cucumber Sauce

3 garlic cloves, minced and divided
$1/2$ teaspoon oregano
$11/2$ pounds ground lamb
Salt and pepper to taste
1 cup sour cream
1 cup chopped seeded cucumber
$1/2$ onion, thinly sliced
4 pita rounds with one-third of the top removed
4 lettuce leaves

Combine two-thirds of the minced garlic, the oregano and lamb in a bowl and mix well. Shape into four patties. Sprinkle with salt and pepper. Place on a grill rack or in a skillet. Grill or fry for 3 to 4 minutes on each side.

To make sauce, combine the sour cream, cucumber, onion, remaining garlic, salt and pepper in a bowl and mix well. Line each pita with the lettuce and cucumber sauce. Add the burgers and serve. **Serves 4.**

*These burgers are so delicious it is worth watching for ground lamb
in your grocery store. Tzatziki is the traditional Greek name
for cucumber sauce.*

Lamb and White Bean Casserole

1 pound dried Great Northern beans	3 bay leaves
8 cups cold water	2 teaspoons essence (see below)
3 pounds boneless leg of lamb, cut into 2-inch chunks	1/4 cup minced garlic
2 teaspoons salt	1 cup chopped peeled tomatoes
2 teaspoons pepper	6 cups chicken stock
2 tablespoons olive oil	1/3 cup chopped green onions
3 cups chopped yellow onions	2 tablespoons chopped parsley
1 1/2 cups chopped celery	1 cup dry bread crumbs
10 sprigs of fresh thyme, tied with twine	1/2 cup (2 ounces) grated Parmesan cheese
	3 tablespoons olive oil

Sort and rinse the beans. Combine with the water in a large saucepan. Cover and bring to a boil. Remove from the heat and let stand for 1 hour. Drain and set aside. Sprinkle the lamb with the salt and pepper. Sauté the lamb in 2 tablespoons olive oil in a skillet until brown on all sides. Remove the lamb from the skillet and set aside.

Cook the onions, celery, thyme, bay leaves and essence for 4 minutes in a large saucepan. Add the garlic and cook for 2 minutes. Add the tomatoes, stock and lamb. Bring to a boil. Reduce the heat and simmer for 30 minutes. Add the beans. Cook for 1 hour or until the beans are tender. The cooking liquid should be thick enough to coat the beans and lamb. If necessary, remove the lamb temporarily and reduce the liquid to the desired consistency. If the liquid is too thick, add additional water. Stir in the green onions and parsley. Discard the bay leaves. Spoon into a 9×13-inch baking dish. Sprinkle with the bread crumbs and cheese. Drizzle with 3 tablespoons olive oil. Bake at 400 degrees for 30 minutes or until golden brown and bubbly. **Serves 12 to 14.**

A fabulous recipe for a crowd. Essence can be made
by mixing 1 1/2 teaspoons each of paprika, salt, and garlic powder
with 3/4 teaspoon each of black pepper, onion powder,
cayenne pepper, oregano, and thyme.

Grilled Pork Tenderloins

3 small pork tenderloins
1/2 cup ketchup
1/2 cup packed brown sugar
1 garlic clove, minced
1 teaspoon chili powder
Juice of 1 lemon
1/4 cup soy sauce
3 tablespoons Worcestershire sauce
1/2 cup chopped onion
1/4 cup water
Salt and pepper to taste

Prick each tenderloin all over with a fork. Place in a large sealable plastic bag. Combine the ketchup, brown sugar, garlic, chili powder, lemon juice, soy sauce, Worcestershire sauce, onion, water, salt and pepper in a saucepan and mix well. Simmer for 15 minutes. Pour over the tenderloins and seal the bag. Marinate in the refrigerator for 24 hours. Drain the tenderloins, discarding the marinade. Place on a grill rack. Grill to 145 degrees on a meat thermometer.* Let stand for 15 minutes before serving. **Serves 8 to 10.**

Penne with Broccoli Rabe and Sausage

2 bunches broccoli rabe
2 pounds sweet Italian sausage
2 tablespoons olive oil
3 garlic cloves, crushed
1/4 teaspoon crushed red pepper flakes
1/2 teaspoon salt
1/2 teaspoon black pepper
1 (14-ounce) can chicken broth
16 ounces penne, cooked al dente
1/2 cup half-and-half (optional)
Grated Parmesan cheese to taste
1/2 cup pine nuts, toasted

Rinse the broccoli rabe and pat dry. Cut into pieces. Cook the sausage in the casings in a skillet until cooked through. Cut the sausage into small pieces. Heat the olive oil in a large skillet. Add the garlic and cook until golden brown. Add the red pepper flakes, salt, black pepper and broccoli rabe to the skillet. Cover and steam for 5 minutes or until the broccoli rabe cooks down. Stir in the broth and sausage. Cook over high heat for 3 minutes or until the sauce reduces slightly. Add the cooked pasta and half-and-half and toss gently. Cook until heated through. Add Parmesan cheese and toss to coat. Add the pine nuts and serve immediately. **Serves 6.**

Pork Tenderloin en Croûte

1 tablespoon Dijon mustard
Thyme to taste
Garlic powder to taste, divided
Salt and pepper to taste
Olive oil
2 pork tenderloins
4 ounces crumbled goat cheese
1 (5-ounce) package arugula
2 plum tomatoes, sliced
1 (17-ounce) package puff pastry
1 egg yolk

Mix the Dijon mustard, thyme, garlic powder, salt and pepper with enough olive oil in a bowl to form a paste. Rub over the tenderloins and place on a rack in a roasting pan. Roast at 425 degrees to 130 degrees on a meat thermometer. Butterfly each tenderloin. Layer the goat cheese, arugula, tomatoes, salt and pepper in the center of each. Fold each tenderloin to enclose the stuffing. Roll the puff pastry into two rectangles. Place one stuffed tenderloin on top of each pastry rectangle. Wrap each with the pastry to enclose, sealing the edges. Place seam side down on a baking sheet. Chill for up to 1 hour. Remove from the refrigerator and brush with a mixture of egg yolk and a small amount of water. Bake at 425 degrees for 35 minutes or until puffed and golden brown. **Serves 8.**

* Note: Recipes in the Meats and Poultry section for pork containing this symbol * do not reflect USDA recommended internal temperatures.

Southwestern Pork Chops

1 cup white rice or brown rice
6 pork rib chops, cut 3/4-inch thick
1 (15-ounce) can Tex-Mex chili beans
2 cups bottled salsa
2 cups frozen whole kernel corn
Fresh cilantro to taste

Cook the rice using the package directions. Trim the pork chops. Coat a 12-inch nonstick skillet with nonstick cooking spray and heat over medium-high heat. Brown the pork chops in batches in the prepared skillet for 2 minutes on each side. Drain 1/2 cup of the liquid from the beans. Combine the beans with the remaining liquid, the salsa and corn in a bowl and mix well. Spoon over the pork chops. Bring to a boil; reduce the heat. Simmer, covered, for 10 minutes or until the pork chops register 150 degrees on a meat thermometer.* Serve over the hot rice and sprinkle with cilantro. **Serves 4 to 6.**

*Quick-cooking rice may be used. Two ears of fresh corn
equal about 1 cup whole kernel corn.*

Spiced Pork Tenderloin with Apples

2 apples
2 pounds boneless pork tenderloin roast
1 tablespoon olive oil
1/4 teaspoon pepper
1 teaspoon ginger, divided
1/2 teaspoon nutmeg, divided
1/2 teaspoon cinnamon, divided
1/2 cup dry white wine
1/4 cup honey
1 tablespoon lemon juice

Peel the apples and cut into wedges. Rub the pork with the olive oil, pepper, 1/2 teaspoon of the ginger, 1/4 teaspoon of the nutmeg and 1/4 teaspoon of the cinnamon. Place the pork in a shallow baking pan. Bake at 350 degrees for 45 minutes or to 155 degrees on a meat thermometer.* Let stand for 10 minutes before slicing. Combine the remaining 1/2 teaspoon ginger, remaining 1/4 teaspoon nutmeg, remaining 1/4 teaspoon cinnamon, the wine, honey and lemon juice in a saucepan and mix well. Add the apple wedges and toss to coat. Simmer over low heat just until the apples are tender. Stir the pork juices into the apples. Cut the pork into slices. Serve with the apples and sauce. **Serves 6 to 8.**

Easy to prepare for a crowd. Apples may be partially cooked several hours before serving. Raisins can be added to the apples.

Osso Buco alla Milanese

6 (1-pound) veal shanks
1¹⁄₂ cups all-purpose flour
Salt and pepper to taste
¹⁄₂ cup olive oil, divided
¹⁄₂ cup (1 stick) unsalted butter
4 cups chopped onions
1¹⁄₂ cups chopped peeled carrots
1¹⁄₂ cups chopped celery
1 cup dry white wine
1 (28-ounce) can diced plum tomatoes
3 to 4 cups beef stock
2 teaspoons minced garlic
2 tablespoons grated lemon zest
5 tablespoons chopped fresh parsley
2 tablespoons grated orange zest (optional)

Secure the veal to the bone with kitchen twine and pat dry. Mix the flour with salt and pepper in a shallow dish. Dredge the veal in the flour mixture to coat. Heat ¹⁄₄ cup of the olive oil in a Dutch oven. Cook the veal in batches for 15 to 20 minutes or until brown on all sides, adding the remaining ¹⁄₄ cup olive oil as needed. Remove to a platter and remove the twine.

Melt the butter in the drippings in the Dutch oven. Add the onions, carrots and celery. Sauté for 15 minutes or until tender. Place the veal on top of the vegetables. Add the wine, tomatoes and stock. Bring to a boil; reduce the heat to low. Simmer, covered, for 1 hour or until very tender and the veal falls from the bones. Combine the garlic, lemon zest, parsley, orange zest, salt and pepper in a bowl to form a gremolata. Sprinkle over the veal. Cook for 5 minutes longer. Serve the veal with the pan sauce. **Serves 6.**

This dish may be served with saffron risotto as the classic accompaniment or with buttered saffron fettuccini. If green peas are in season, add them to the rice or noodles. Lamb may be substituted for the veal. The veal may be simmered in a 350-degree oven.

Sherried Veal and Olives

1¹/₂ pounds veal scallopini
Salt and pepper to taste
¹/₄ cup olive oil, divided
1 large onion, chopped
1 green bell pepper, chopped
3 garlic cloves, minced
6 ounces fresh mushrooms, sliced
1 (14-ounce) can diced tomatoes
8 large Spanish olives, chopped
4 ounces ham, cut into ¹/₄-inch cubes
2 tablespoons all-purpose flour
¹/₃ cup dry sherry
¹/₃ cup water
2 cups cooked rice

Pat the veal dry and pound ¹/₄ inch thick. Season lightly with salt and pepper. Heat
2 tablespoons of the olive oil in a large skillet over medium-low heat. Add the veal. Cook
for 2 minutes on each side or until light brown. Remove the veal from the skillet and set
aside. Add the remaining 2 tablespoons olive oil to the pan drippings in the skillet. Add the
onion, bell pepper and garlic. Sauté for 5 minutes or until soft. Stir in the mushrooms,
tomatoes, olives, ham and flour. Cook for 5 minutes longer. Add the sherry and water. Bring
to a boil. Reduce the heat and simmer for 3 to 4 minutes. Layer the veal on top of the
vegetable mixture. Cook until the veal is heated through. Serve over the rice. **Serves 4.**

*This dish may be prepared in advance, chilled, and then
reheated for a short time in the oven until warm. Thinly sliced
chicken may be substituted for the veal.*

Veal Pierre

12 (2- to 3-ounce) medallions of veal scallopini
Salt and pepper to taste
1/2 cup all-purpose flour
2 tablespoons butter
3 shallots, chopped
1 cup dry white wine
1 to 1 1/2 cups heavy cream
2 avocados, chopped
1 1/2 teaspoons tarragon
1 cup (4 ounces) shredded Swiss cheese
Chopped fresh parsley for garnish

Pound the veal thin and season with salt and pepper. Dredge in the flour to coat. Sauté the veal in the butter in a skillet until brown. Remove to an ovenproof serving platter. Sauté the shallots in the pan drippings. Add the wine. Cook until the liquid is reduced by one-fourth. Add the cream. Cook until the liquid is reduced by one-half or until the sauce coats the back of a spoon. Adjust the seasonings to taste. Add the avocados and tarragon. Cook for 2 minutes. Pour over the veal. Top with the cheese. Broil until bubbly and the cheese melts. Garnish with the parsley and serve immediately. **Serves 6.**

Don't let the avocado fool you, because this is very special.
Chicken may be substituted for the veal.

Balsamic Chicken

4 boneless skinless chicken breasts
1/2 cup Newman's Own Balsamic Dressing
3 tablespoons olive oil
1 onion, cut into thin slices
1 (14-ounce) can diced tomatoes, drained
1/2 cup vermouth
Salt and pepper to taste

Cut the chicken crosswise into halves to make eight thin pieces. Place in a sealable plastic bag. Add the dressing and seal the bag. Marinate in the refrigerator for 2 to 3 hours. Drain the chicken, discarding the marinade. Sauté the chicken in the olive oil in a large skillet for 3 to 4 minutes on each side. Remove to a plate. Cover and keep warm. Add the onion and tomatoes to the pan drippings, stirring to scrape up the brown bits. Add the vermouth, salt and pepper. Cook for 3 to 4 minutes. Return the chicken to the skillet. Cook for 2 minutes or until the chicken is cooked through. Serve with mashed potatoes or rice. **Serves 4 to 6.**

Grape tomato halves may be substituted for the canned tomatoes.

Chicken Enchiladas

2 large onions, thinly sliced
2 tablespoons butter
2 cups chopped cooked chicken
1/2 cup chopped roasted red peppers
6 ounces cream cheese, cut into cubes
1/4 teaspoon salt
1/4 teaspoon pepper
4 (4-ounce) cans diced green chiles
1 small onion, chopped
2 garlic cloves, minced
2 teaspoons oregano
1 teaspoon ground cumin
1/2 teaspoon sugar
1 (14-ounce) can chicken broth
1/2 cup salsa
8 (7-inch) flour tortillas
1 to 2 cups (4 to 8 ounces) shredded Cheddar cheese

Sauté the sliced onions in the butter in a large skillet for 20 minutes or until caramelized. Reduce the heat. Stir in the chicken. Add the roasted red peppers, cream cheese, salt and pepper and mix well. Remove from the heat and set aside.

Pulse the green chiles, chopped onion, garlic, oregano, cumin and sugar in a food processor until blended. Spoon into a saucepan and add the broth. Bring to a boil. Boil for 5 minutes or until slightly thickened to the consistency of thin gravy. Remove from the heat. Stir in the salsa.

Spread one-third of the green chile mixture in a lightly buttered 9×13-inch baking dish. Spoon the chicken mixture down the center of each tortilla and roll up. Place seam side down in the prepared baking dish. Top with the remaining green chile mixture and sprinkle with the Cheddar cheese. Bake at 375 degrees for 20 minutes. **Serves 4 to 6.**

Chicken Hash

6 potatoes
1/2 cup olive oil, divided
1 onion, chopped
1 red bell pepper, chopped
2 garlic cloves, minced
2 tablespoons chopped fresh thyme leaves (optional)
1 teaspoon paprika
1 tablespoon tomato paste
1 teaspoon kosher salt
1 teaspoon pepper
3 cups cubed cooked chicken
Sour cream for garnish
Shredded Cheddar cheese for garnish

Cut the potatoes into 1/4-inch cubes. Heat 1/4 cup of the olive oil in a large skillet over medium-low heat. Add the potatoes in batches a single layer at a time. Fry each batch for 10 to 15 minutes or until evenly brown and cooked through. Remove the potatoes to an ovenproof platter and keep warm in a 200-degree oven.

Heat the remaining 1/4 cup olive oil with the drippings in the skillet. Add the onion. Cook over low heat for 10 minutes or until caramelized. Add the bell pepper. Sauté over high heat for 2 minutes. Reduce the heat and add the garlic, thyme, paprika, tomato paste, kosher salt and pepper. Add the chicken. Cook until heated through, stirring constantly. Return the potatoes to the skillet and stir to mix. Spoon onto a serving platter. Garnish with dollops of sour cream and shredded Cheddar cheese. **Serves 6.**

An easy dish to make using purchased rotisserie chicken.

Florentine Chicken Lasagna

6 lasagna noodles
2 (10-ounce) packages frozen chopped spinach, thawed
2 cups chopped cooked chicken
2 cups (8 ounces) shredded Cheddar cheese
1/3 cup finely chopped onion
1 teaspoon nutmeg
1 tablespoon cornstarch
1 teaspoon salt
1/2 teaspoon pepper
1 tablespoon soy sauce
1 (10-ounce) can cream of mushroom soup
1 cup sour cream
8 ounces fresh mushrooms, sliced
1/3 cup mayonnaise
1/4 cup (1/2 stick) butter
1 cup chopped pecans
1 cup (4 ounces) grated Parmesan cheese

Cook the noodles using the package directions. Drain and set aside. Drain the spinach and squeeze dry. Combine the spinach, chicken, Cheddar cheese, onion, nutmeg, cornstarch, salt, pepper, soy sauce, soup, sour cream, mushrooms and mayonnaise in a large bowl and mix well. Melt the butter in a small skillet. Add the pecans and sauté until toasted.

Arrange three of the noodles in a lightly buttered 9×13-inch baking dish. Spread one-half of the chicken mixture over the noodles. Repeat the layers with the remaining three noodles and the remaining chicken mixture. Sprinkle with the Parmesan cheese and pecans. Bake, covered, at 350 degrees for 55 to 60 minutes or until hot and bubbly. Let stand for 15 minutes before serving. **Serves 8 to 10.**

Greek Chicken Breasts

6 boneless skinless chicken breasts
Salt and pepper to taste
1 (10-ounce) package frozen chopped spinach, thawed
8 ounces crumbled feta cheese
1/2 cup mayonnaise
1 garlic clove, minced
1/4 cup all-purpose flour
1/2 teaspoon paprika
12 slices bacon

Cut a pocket into each chicken breast. Sprinkle with salt and pepper. Drain the spinach and squeeze dry. Combine the spinach, cheese, mayonnaise and garlic in a bowl and mix well. Stuff equally into the chicken pockets. Mix the flour and paprika in a shallow dish. Dredge the chicken in the flour mixture. Wrap each chicken breast with two slices of the bacon. Place on a rack in a baking dish. Bake at 325 degrees for 1 hour. **Serves 6.**

Indian Chicken Curry

1 **pound boneless chicken breasts**
2 **tablespoons curry powder**
1/4 **teaspoon cinnamon**
2 **tablespoons olive oil, divided**
1 **yellow onion, thinly sliced**
2 **zucchini, thinly sliced**
1 1/2 **cups chicken broth**
1 1/2 **cups heavy cream**
1 1/2 **teaspoons kosher salt**
1/4 **teaspoon pepper**
2 **cups cooked white rice**
1/2 **cup fresh basil leaves, julienned for garnish**
1/4 **cup cashews, coarsely chopped for garnish**

Cut the chicken into 1-inch pieces. Mix the curry powder and cinnamon in a bowl. Add the chicken and toss to coat. Heat 1 tablespoon of the olive oil in a large skillet over medium heat. Add the onion and zucchini. Sauté for 3 to 5 minutes or until soft. Remove the vegetables to a plate. Heat the remaining 1 tablespoon olive oil with the pan drippings. Add the chicken. Cook for 5 minutes or until brown on all sides. Add the broth, cream, kosher salt and pepper. Bring to a simmer. Return the vegetables to the skillet. Cook for 5 to 7 minutes or until the chicken is cooked through. Divide the rice among four individual serving bowls and top with the curry. Garnish with the basil and cashews. **Serves 4.**

Parmesan Chicken with Arugula

4 boneless skinless chicken breasts
3/4 cup (3 ounces) grated Parmesan cheese
3/4 cup dry bread crumbs
2 eggs, beaten
1 teaspoon finely chopped fresh rosemary
2 garlic cloves, crushed
1/2 cup olive oil
2 bunches arugula
1 head radicchio
1 red onion, thinly sliced
4 plum tomatoes, cut into chunks
1/4 cup extra-virgin olive oil
1 tablespoon balsamic vinegar
1 lemon, cut into wedges for garnish

Cut the chicken breasts crosswise into halves to make eight thin pieces. Pound the chicken 1/4 inch thick. Mix the cheese and bread crumbs in a shallow dish. Dredge the chicken in the bread crumb mixture. Dip into the eggs and dredge again in the bread crumb mixture. Sauté the rosemary and garlic in 1/2 cup olive oil in a large skillet. Remove the rosemary and garlic from the pan and discard. Add the chicken to the flavored oil in the skillet. Cook until brown on each side and the juices run clear. Arrange the chicken on four serving plates.

Rinse the arugula and pat dry. Tear the radicchio into large pieces. Toss the arugula, radicchio, red onion and tomatoes with 1/4 cup olive oil and the balsamic vinegar in a bowl. Divide evenly over the chicken. Garnish with lemon wedges. **Serves 4.**

Veal scallopini or pork tenderloin may be substituted for the chicken.

Poblano Chicken

2 large Poblano chiles
$1/2$ cup brown rice
1 (14-ounce) can petite-diced tomatoes
$1/4$ teaspoon salt
$1/2$ teaspoon chili powder
4 boneless skinless chicken breasts
1 tablespoon olive oil
1 onion, chopped
$1/2$ cup sour cream
$2^{1/2}$ cups (10 ounces) shredded Colby Jack cheese

Remove the seeds and veins from the Poblano chiles. Chop the Poblano chiles. Combine the rice, tomatoes, salt and chili powder in a saucepan and mix well. Cook for 40 minutes, adding water if the rice needs additional liquid as it cooks. Brown the chicken in the olive oil in a skillet. Do not cook through. Remove the chicken from the skillet using a slotted spoon and set aside.

Cook the Poblano chiles and onion in the drippings in the skillet for 2 to 4 minutes or until soft. Remove from the heat. Stir in the sour cream. Layer the rice mixture and chicken in a 9×9-inch baking dish. Pour the Poblano chile sauce over the chicken. Top with the cheese. Bake at 325 degrees for 25 minutes. **Serves 4.**

*White rice may be used instead of the brown rice; cook for only
30 minutes. No other liquid is needed to cook the rice.*

Provençal Chicken Thighs

1 tablespoon fresh thyme
1¹/2 teaspoons salt, divided
Pepper to taste
All-purpose flour for dusting
4 to 6 boneless skinless chicken thighs
1 to 2 tablespoons olive oil
¹/2 cup vermouth
2 cups thinly sliced onions
1 garlic clove, minced
1 (14-ounce) can plum tomatoes
¹/4 cup fresh basil
¹/2 teaspoon sugar
1 teaspoon oregano
Hot cooked rice or pasta

Mix the thyme, 1 teaspoon of the salt, pepper and flour in a small bowl. Dredge the chicken in the flour mixture. Sauté the chicken in the olive oil in a large skillet for 3 minutes on each side. Remove the chicken from the skillet. Add the vermouth to the pan drippings, stirring to scrape up the brown bits. Stir in the onions and garlic. Cook until wilted. Add the tomatoes and basil. Stir in the remaining ¹/2 teaspoon salt, the pepper, sugar and oregano. Cook over medium heat for 5 minutes. Return the chicken to the skillet. Cover and cook over medium heat for 30 to 40 minutes or until the chicken is cooked through. Serve over hot cooked rice or pasta. **Serves 4.**

Roasted Cornish Hens with Fruit Salsa

2 (1³/₄-pound) Cornish game hens
1¹/₂ cups bottled fruit salsa
3 tablespoons chopped fresh thyme
1 teaspoon hot pepper sauce
2 tablespoons olive oil
1¹/₂ teaspoons ground allspice
Salt and pepper to taste

Split each hen along the backbone into halves. Mix the salsa, thyme and hot sauce in a medium bowl. Combine 3 tablespoons of the salsa mixture with the olive oil and allspice in a small bowl. Place the hens on a rack on a baking sheet. Season with salt and pepper. Brush with the olive oil mixture. Roast at 450 degrees for 25 minutes or until the juices run clear when the thigh is pierced. Remove to serving plates. Spoon the salsa mixture over the top. **Serves 4.**

Peach or mango salsa would be a nice variation.

Sun-Dried Tomato and Artichoke Chicken

1½ pounds boneless skinless chicken breasts

¼ cup all-purpose flour

2 tablespoons canola oil

½ cup white wine

Juice of ½ lemon

1 (14-ounce) can quartered artichoke hearts, drained

½ cup julienned sun-dried tomatoes in oil

2 tablespoons unsalted butter

½ teaspoon kosher salt

⅛ teaspoon pepper

6 to 8 sprigs of fresh thyme leaves

2 tablespoons grated Parmesan cheese

Cut the chicken into 1-inch chunks. Place in a sealable plastic bag and add the flour. Seal the bag and shake to coat. Discard any excess flour. Sauté the chicken in the oil in a large skillet for 2 to 3 minutes on each side until the chicken begins to brown. Stir in the wine. Cook over medium-low heat for 2 to 3 minutes or until the liquid is slightly reduced. Pour the lemon juice over the chicken. Stir in the artichoke hearts, sun-dried tomatoes, butter, kosher salt and pepper. Cover and cook for 2 to 3 minutes. Remove from the heat. Stir in the thyme. Sprinkle with Parmesan cheese before serving. **Serves 4 to 6.**

Supreme Chicken Casserole

3 cups chopped cooked chicken
2 or 3 hard-cooked eggs, chopped
2 cups cooked rice
1½ cups chopped celery
1 small onion, chopped
1 cup mayonnaise
2 (10-ounce) cans cream of mushroom soup
1 (3-ounce) package slivered almonds, toasted
1 teaspoon salt
2 tablespoons lemon juice
1 cup crumbled Cheez-Its
2 tablespoons butter, melted

Mix the chicken, eggs, rice, celery, onion, mayonnaise, soup, almonds, salt and lemon juice in a large bowl. Spoon into a buttered 9×13-inch baking dish. Mix the Cheez-Its and butter together. Sprinkle over the chicken mixture. Chill, covered, for 8 to 10 hours. Remove from the refrigerator and let stand for 1 hour. Bake at 350 degrees for 40 to 45 minutes or until heated through. **Serves 8 to 10.**

*This recipe always brings rave reviews. For topping variation,
mix 1 cup bread crumbs with ¼ cup shredded
Cheddar cheese and the melted butter. This casserole may be frozen.
Add the topping before baking.*

Tandoori Chicken

Tomato Cucumber Raita

2 pickling cucumbers, peeled, seeded and finely chopped
1 small Roma tomato, seeded and chopped
1 cup plain yogurt
1/4 cup minced red onion
2 tablespoons chopped fresh mint
1/4 teaspoon ground cumin
1/4 teaspoon salt, or to taste
1/8 teaspoon white pepper
1/8 teaspoon cayenne pepper

Chicken

1 teaspoon paprika
1 teaspoon coriander
1/2 teaspoon chili powder
1/4 teaspoon ground cumin
1/4 teaspoon salt
1/4 teaspoon pepper
Pinch of nutmeg
8 boneless skinless chicken breasts, split
2 tablespoons vegetable oil

To prepare the raita, combine the cucumbers, tomato, yogurt, onion, mint, cumin, salt, white pepper and cayenne pepper in a bowl and mix well.

To prepare the chicken, mix the paprika, coriander, chili powder, cumin, salt, pepper and nutmeg in a bowl and mix well. Pound the chicken 1/4 inch thick. Brush the oil on both sides. Season with the paprika mixture on both sides. Place on a grill rack. Grill over medium-high heat for 3 to 4 minutes on each side or until cooked through. Serve warm with the raita. **Serves 6 to 8.**

Duck Ragù

3 pounds boneless skinless duck pieces
3/4 teaspoon salt
1/2 teaspoon pepper
3 tablespoons olive oil
1 onion, chopped
2 garlic cloves, minced
1 teaspoon red pepper flakes (optional)
1 carrot, chopped
1 rib celery, chopped
2 tablespoons tomato paste
1 1/2 cups red wine
1 (28-ounce) can diced tomatoes
1 teaspoon sugar
8 ounces fresh mushrooms, sliced
1 teaspoon thyme
12 ounces pappardelle pasta, cooked
Chopped parsley for garnish

Trim the excess fat from the duck pieces. Rub with a mixture of the salt and pepper. Heat the olive oil in a skillet. Add the duck pieces in batches and sauté for 10 minutes or until cooked through. Remove the duck from the skillet. Add the onion and garlic to the drippings in the skillet and cook until softened. Stir in the red pepper flakes. Add the carrot, celery and tomato paste and cook for 2 minutes. Add the wine, stirring to scrape up the brown bits. Stir in the tomatoes, sugar, mushrooms and thyme. Bring to a boil. Place the duck pieces in a Dutch oven. Pour the hot tomato sauce over the duck. Cook, covered, over low heat for 2 1/2 hours or until the duck is tender. Remove the duck and shred into bite-size pieces. Return to the sauce. Cook, covered, for 20 minutes. Adjust the seasonings to taste. Spoon over the cooked pasta. Garnish with parsley. **Serves 6 to 8.**

*Ragù may be cooked in a slow cooker on High
for 3 1/2 hours or on Low for 7 1/2 hours. Wide noodles
may be substituted for the pappardelle.*

Duck Risotto

1 frozen whole duck, thawed
2 cups red wine
4 cups duck stock
1 cup chopped onion
2 teaspoons olive oil
1^1/$_2$ cups arborio rice
^{1}/$_3$ cup vermouth
2 cups frozen green peas, thawed
3 tablespoons grated Parmesan cheese

Place the duck and wine in a Dutch oven. Braise, covered, at 325 degrees for 3 hours. Remove the duck from the pan, reserving the liquid. Shred the duck, discarding the skin and bones. Skim the fat from the surface of the stock and pour the stock into a saucepan. Keep warm over low heat.

Sauté the onion in the olive oil in a large Dutch oven for 4 minutes or until golden brown. Add the rice and sauté for 30 seconds. Stir in the vermouth. Cook for 45 seconds or until the liquid is nearly absorbed, stirring constantly. Stir in 1 cup of the stock. Cook until the stock is nearly absorbed, stirring constantly. Continue to stir in the stock ^{1}/$_2$ cup at a time, stirring constantly and cooking for 20 minutes after each addition or until the rice is tender. Remove from the heat. Stir in the peas, cheese and 2 cups or more of the shredded duck. Serve immediately. **Serves 4.**

Homemade duck stock makes this recipe a winner.
Extra stock can be made by covering duck bones with water. Bring to
a boil. Reduce the heat and simmer for 2 hours. Chicken stock may be
added to duck stock to make enough liquid, if desired.

Turkey and Fusilli Bake

8 ounces fusilli pasta
1 pound ground turkey
1 onion, chopped
1 (26-ounce) jar marinara sauce
32 ounces ricotta cheese
3 eggs, beaten
2 tablespoons chopped parsley
1/4 cup (1 ounce) grated Parmesan cheese
2 cups (8 ounces) shredded mozzarella cheese, divided

Cook the pasta until al dente using the package directions. Brown the ground turkey in a skillet, stirring until crumbly. Add the onion. Cook for 7 minutes. Add the marinara sauce and bring to a simmer. Combine the ricotta cheese, eggs, parsley, Parmesan cheese and 1/2 cup of the mozzarella cheese in a bowl and mix well. Layer one-half of the pasta, one-half of the sauce, the ricotta cheese mixture, the remaining pasta, the remaining sauce and the remaining 1 1/2 cups mozzarella cheese in a 9×13-inch baking dish coated with nonstick cooking spray. Cover with foil and place on a baking sheet. Bake at 350 degrees for 55 minutes. Remove the foil and bake until the mozzarella cheese begins to brown. Let stand for 10 to 15 minutes before serving. **Serves 8.**

Turkey Meatballs and Pasta

1 pound rotini pasta
3 tablespoons olive oil
1 cup finely minced onion, divided
1¼ teaspoons salt, divided
3/4 teaspoon pepper, divided
8 ounces fresh mushrooms, sliced
2 tablespoons all-purpose flour
2½ cups chicken broth
1/4 cup dry bread crumbs
1/3 cup milk
1 cup (4 ounces) grated Parmesan cheese, divided
1 egg
1 pound ground turkey
2 garlic cloves, minced
3 tablespoons minced flat-leaf parsley
2/3 cup heavy cream

Cook the pasta using the package directions; drain. Heat the olive oil in a large skillet over medium heat. Add 1/2 cup of the onion, 1/4 teaspoon of the salt, 1/4 teaspoon of the pepper and the mushrooms and cook for 5 minutes. Add the flour. Cook for 2 minutes, stirring constantly. Add the broth. Simmer, covered, for 10 minutes.

Soak the bread crumbs in the milk in a small bowl for 10 minutes. Mix the remaining 1/2 cup onion, 1/2 cup of the cheese, remaining 1 teaspoon salt, remaining 1/2 teaspoon pepper, the egg, ground turkey, garlic and parsley in a bowl. Stir in the bread crumb mixture. Shape into 1 1/2-inch meatballs. Add to the sauce. Simmer, covered, for 20 minutes. Add the cream and return to a simmer. Add the remaining 1/2 cup cheese. Cook until slightly thickened, stirring constantly. Add the pasta and toss gently to coat. Serve with additional cheese, if desired. **Serves 4 to 6.**

The turkey mixture would make great hamburgers or meat loaf.

Seafood

Fishing boats are a common and delightful sight in our harbor, and the island offers a variety of fishing and boating options, both fresh and salt water. Fernandina Beach is known as the birthplace of the modern offshore shrimping industry, and the island has provided a large percentage of Florida's Atlantic white shrimp. Our waters produce a bountiful harvest and have an historic and colorful past.

Barbecued Salmon

2 tablespoons soy sauce
1 teaspoon sherry
Pinch of cayenne pepper
1 teaspoon Worcestershire sauce
1/2 teaspoon Tabasco sauce, divided
3 tablespoons white wine, divided
2 tablespoons plus 1 teaspoon lemon juice
2 tablespoons chopped fresh ginger
1/2 teaspoon granulated sugar
3 garlic cloves, minced and divided
4 (6- to 8-ounce) salmon fillets
1/4 cup (1/2 stick) butter
1 onion, chopped
1/4 cup packed brown sugar
2 tablespoons grated fresh ginger
1/4 teaspoon salt

Mix the soy sauce, sherry, cayenne pepper, Worcestershire sauce, 1/4 teaspoon of the Tabasco sauce, 1 tablespoon of the white wine, 1 teaspoon of the lemon juice, the chopped ginger, granulated sugar and two-thirds of the garlic in a bowl. Place the salmon in a sealable plastic bag. Add the marinade and seal the bag. Marinate in the refrigerator for 1 to 2 hours.

Melt the butter in a skillet. Add the onion and sauté until soft but not brown. Add the brown sugar, the remaining 2 tablespoons lemon juice, the remaining 2 tablespoons white wine, the remaining one-third garlic, the remaining 1/4 teaspoon Tabasco sauce, the grated ginger and salt. Simmer for 10 minutes.

Place the salmon with the marinade in an ovenproof skillet. Simmer, covered, for 10 minutes. Spoon one-half of the sauce over the salmon. Simmer, covered, for 2 minutes. Broil, uncovered, for 2 to 3 minutes or until the salmon flakes easily. Serve the remaining sauce on the side. **Serves 4.**

Gingered Tuna

Ginger Sauce
1 small shallot, minced
1 tablespoon grated fresh ginger
Pepper to taste
1/3 cup soy sauce
1/4 cup lime juice
1 to 2 tablespoons sugar
1/4 cup olive oil

Tuna
1/2 cup minced fresh ginger
1/4 cup sesame seeds
1 tablespoon cracked pepper
1 pound fresh tuna
Kosher salt to taste
3 tablespoons peanut oil
1 tablespoon lime juice

To prepare the sauce, combine the shallot, ginger, pepper, soy sauce, lime juice and sugar in a bowl. Whisk in the olive oil.

To prepare the tuna, mix the ginger, sesame seeds and pepper on a shallow plate. Sprinkle the tuna with salt. Press into the ginger mixture to cover both sides. Sear the tuna in the peanut oil in a large skillet for 30 seconds on each side. Remove the tuna to a plate. Add the lime juice to the drippings in the skillet, stirring to scrape up the brown bits. Pour over the tuna. Cut into bite-size pieces and drizzle with the ginger sauce. **Serves 6.**

This is great as an appetizer and will serve ten to twelve.
Over greens as a salad, it serves six.

Individual Parchment Fillets

Sweet potato or white potato slices
Salt and pepper to taste
Fresh baby spinach
Chopped green onions
Julienned carrots
2 (6-ounce) fish fillets, skin removed
Melted butter
Capers to taste
2 thin slices lemon

Preheat a baking sheet in a 400-degree oven. Cut baking parchment into two 15×18-inch sheets. Layer a few potato slices in the center of each sheet. Sprinkle with salt and pepper. Add spinach, green onions and carrots to each. Layer the fish over the vegetables and sprinkle with salt and pepper. Drizzle with melted butter. Top with capers and a lemon slice. Bring the baking parchment together over the fish. Fold the top down and tuck the ends under. Place the packets on the hot baking sheet. Bake at 400 degrees for 20 minutes. **Serves 2.**

To serve without the baking parchment, layer all of the ingredients in a buttered baking dish and bake as directed. Most fish fillets can be used. For variation, season the fish with lemon pepper and salt. Top with coarsely chopped sun-dried tomatoes, sliced black olives, feta cheese, and toasted pine nuts. Bake as directed.

Poached Salmon with Vegetable Salad

Dill Sauce

1/3 cup mayonnaise

1/3 cup plain yogurt

1/3 cup sour cream

3 tablespoons chopped fresh dill weed

3 tablespoons chopped fresh basil

2 teaspoons Dijon mustard

3 tablespoons chopped green onions

Curry powder to taste

Poached Salmon with Vegetable Salad

6 cups water

2 tablespoons fresh lemon juice

1 cup celery leaves

3/4 teaspoon salt

4 to 6 salmon fillets, skin removed

12 whole mushrooms, cut into quarters

2 tomatoes, coarsely chopped

1 cup (1/4-inch-thick) cucumber slices, cut into halves

1/2 cup sliced celery

2 tablespoons chopped green onions

Bottled vinaigrette to taste

4 to 6 lemon slices for garnish

To prepare the dill sauce, combine the mayonnaise, yogurt, sour cream, dill weed, basil, Dijon mustard, green onions and curry powder in a bowl and mix well.

To prepare the salmon, bring the water, lemon juice, celery leaves and salt to a boil in a large skillet. Reduce the heat and simmer for 15 minutes. Add the salmon. Cook for 12 minutes or until the salmon flakes easily. Cool the salmon in the liquid until room temperature. Drain and chill in the refrigerator.

For the salad, combine the mushrooms, tomatoes, cucumbers, celery and green onions in a bowl. Add vinaigrette and toss to coat. Place on a serving platter. Top with the salmon and dill sauce. Garnish with the lemon slices. **Serves 4 to 6.**

Roasted Salmon with Cucumber Sour Cream

1 cup baby spinach leaves
1 cup arugula leaves
1/2 shallot
1/2 cup chopped seeded peeled cucumber
3/4 cup sour cream
3 tablespoons Dijon mustard
Salt and pepper to taste
1/3 cup white wine
1/3 cup orange juice
1/3 cup soy sauce
1 pound salmon fillets

To make cucumber sour cream, process the spinach, arugula, shallot and cucumber in a food processor until chopped. Add the sour cream and Dijon mustard and mix well. Sprinkle with salt and pepper. Chill, covered, in the refrigerator.

Combine the wine, orange juice and soy sauce in a bowl and mix well. Place the salmon in a sealable plastic bag. Add the marinade. Marinate in the refrigerator for 2 hours. Drain the salmon, discarding the marinade. Arrange the salmon skin side down in a 9×13-inch baking dish lined with Reynolds release foil. Roast at 450 degrees for 14 minutes or until the salmon is opaque in the center. Top with the cucumber sour cream. **Serves 2 or 3.**

*Serve the salmon and cucumber sour cream
over sugar snap peas as a salad.*

Salmon Fillet with Yogurt Sauce

Olive oil
2 (8-ounce) salmon fillets
1 teaspoon fresh dill weed, divided
1/2 teaspoon garlic powder, divided
1 white onion, sliced
Coarsely ground pepper to taste
1/4 cup dry white wine
1 cup plain yogurt
Chopped fresh parsley for garnish
1 lemon, cut into quarters for garnish

Brush olive oil on the skinless side of the salmon. Sprinkle with 1/4 teaspoon of the dill weed and 1/4 teaspoon of the garlic powder. Cover the bottom of a nonstick skillet with the onion. Place the salmon skin side up over the onion and brush lightly with olive oil. Sprinkle with 1/4 teaspoon of the remaining dill weed, the remaining 1/4 teaspoon garlic powder and pepper. Add the wine. Bring to a simmer. Cover and cook for 10 minutes per inch of thickness of the salmon or until the salmon flakes easily and is pink. Remove and discard the skin. Mix the yogurt and remaining 1/2 teaspoon dill weed in a bowl.

To serve hot, cover the salmon with a thin layer of the yogurt sauce. Garnish with parsley and lemon. Serve with the remaining yogurt sauce on the side.

To serve cold, cover the salmon with 1/4 to 1/2 inch of the yogurt sauce and chill in the refrigerator. When ready to serve, garnish with parsley and lemon. Serve with toasted thin bread rounds. **Serves 2.**

Snapper with Crab Meat and Shrimp

2 (6-ounce) snapper fillets	2 teaspoons
All-purpose flour	Worcestershire sauce
7 tablespoons butter, divided	1/2 cup white wine
4 jumbo shrimp, peeled	2 teaspoons fresh lemon juice
and deveined	2 shallots, chopped
1 (6-ounce) can lump crab meat	2 teaspoons chopped
1 tablespoon Cajun seasoning	fresh parsley

Dredge the snapper in flour. Melt 3 tablespoons of the butter in a medium skillet over high heat. Add the snapper and sauté until done. Sauté the shrimp and crab meat in another skillet. Sprinkle with the Cajun seasoning. Cook for 5 to 8 minutes or until light brown. Add the Worcestershire sauce, wine, lemon juice, shallots and parsley. Cook for 5 minutes or until the liquid is reduced. Remove the snapper to a warm plate. Top with the shrimp and crab meat. Whisk the remaining 4 tablespoons butter into the pan juices in the skillet until melted. Pour over the seafood. **Serves 2.**

Wasabi-Glazed Tilapia

2 tablespoons soy sauce	1 teaspoon sesame oil
1/2 teaspoon wasabi powder, or	1/2 teaspoon sugar
to taste	4 (4- to 6-ounce) tilapia fillets

Combine the soy sauce, wasabi powder, sesame oil and sugar in a bowl and mix well. Place the tilapia in a lightly buttered 8×8-inch baking dish and brush generously with the marinade. Place on a rack in a broiler pan or on a grill rack. Broil or grill for 6 minutes. Turn and brush with the remaining marinade. Broil or grill for 5 minutes longer or until the tilapia flakes easily. **Serves 4.**

Grouper, halibut, or flounder may be substituted for
the tilapia. Light and tasty.

Crab Cakes with Red Pepper Mayonnaise

Red Pepper Mayonnaise

1 red bell pepper
1/2 cup mayonnaise
1 garlic clove
Dash of Tabasco sauce

Crab Cakes

1/2 cup mayonnaise
1/4 cup minced red onion
1/4 cup minced red bell pepper
2 tablespoons minced celery
1 1/2 teaspoons fresh lemon juice
1 egg white, beaten
1 pound lump crab meat, shells removed
1 1/4 cups panko, divided
2 tablespoons butter
10 cups trimmed watercress (about 10 ounces)

To prepare the red pepper mayonnaise, cut the bell pepper lengthwise into halves, discarding the seeds and membranes. Place the bell pepper halves skin side up on a foil-lined baking sheet and flatten with your hand. Broil for 12 minutes or until blackened. Place in a plastic bag and seal. Let stand for 10 minutes; peel. Process the roasted bell pepper, mayonnaise, garlic and Tabasco sauce in a food processor until smooth. Spoon into a serving bowl. Chill, covered, in the refrigerator.

To prepare the crab cakes, combine the mayonnaise, red onion, bell pepper, celery, lemon juice, egg white, crab meat and 3/4 cup of the bread crumbs in a large bowl and mix well. Shape into six patties. Dredge in the remaining 1/2 cup bread crumbs. Chill in the refrigerator. Sauté the patties in the butter in a large skillet for 10 minutes or until light brown, turning once. Serve on the watercress with the red pepper mayonnaise. **Serves 6.**

Fernandina Seafood Stew

2 tablespoons extra-virgin olive oil
1 red bell pepper, thinly sliced
1 green bell pepper, thinly sliced
1 sweet onion, thinly sliced
1 tablespoon crushed garlic
1 dozen large shrimp, peeled and deveined
12 ounces fresh white fish
12 mussels
12 clams
1 cup white wine
2 teaspoons fresh thyme
4 to 5 cups Knorr fish broth
1 (5-ounce) package couscous, cooked
Sprigs of thyme for garnish

Heat the olive oil in a Dutch oven. Add the bell peppers, onion and garlic. Sauté for 2 to 3 minutes or until soft. Add the shrimp and fish. Sauté for 2 to 3 minutes. Add the mussels, clams and wine. Cook, covered, for 3 minutes or until the shellfish steam open. Discard any shellfish that do not open. Add 2 teaspoons thyme and the broth. Cook until heated through. Place 1/2 cup of the couscous in each of four individual serving bowls. Divide the seafood and broth accordingly into the bowls. Garnish with sprigs of thyme and serve with baguettes. **Serves 4.**

Green Risotto with Lobster

5 cups chicken stock	1 cup fresh spinach leaves
1/2 cup olive oil	4 (5-ounce) lobster tails, cooked
1 onion, finely chopped	Olive oil for sautéing
1 1/2 cups arborio rice	Grated Parmesan cheese to taste
1/2 cup white wine	

Heat the stock in a saucepan; keep warm. Heat 1/2 cup olive oil in a heavy 3-quart saucepan. Add the onion and sauté until golden brown. Add the rice and sauté for 30 seconds. Stir in 1 cup of the stock. Cook until the liquid is nearly absorbed, stirring constantly. Stir in the wine. Continue to add the stock 1/2 cup at a time and cook until each portion is absorbed before adding the next, stirring constantly. Cook for 20 minutes or until the rice is al dente. Rinse the spinach leaves. Purée the wet spinach leaves in a food processor. Stir into the rice. Cut the lobster into chunks. Sauté in olive oil in a small skillet until heated through. Stir into the risotto. Sprinkle with Parmesan cheese and serve immediately. **Serves 6.**

Grits with Shrimp and Greens

2 cups milk	1/4 to 1/2 cup (1/2 to 1 stick) butter
2 cups water	1 to 2 pounds shrimp, peeled
1 cup regular grits	and deveined
1 garlic clove, chopped	10 ounces arugula, rinsed and
1 to 2 cups (4 to 8 ounces)	trimmed
grated Parmigiano-	Salt and pepper to taste
Reggiano cheese	Chopped parsley for garnish

Bring the milk and water to a simmer in a large saucepan over medium heat. Add the grits and garlic. Bring to a boil. Cook until soft and creamy. Stir in the cheese and butter. Add the shrimp. Cook until the shrimp turn pink. Fold in the arugula and remove from the heat. Add salt and pepper. Garnish with parsley. **Serves 4 to 6.**

Baby spinach may be substituted for the arugula.

Lasagna Frutta di Mare

Béchamel Sauce
1/4 cup (1/2 stick) butter
1/4 cup all-purpose flour
2 cups milk
Salt and pepper to taste

Lasagna
1 tablespoon butter
1 tablespoon shallots, chopped
1 1/2 pounds fresh shrimp, peeled, deveined and cut into halves
1 pound bay scallops, cut into quarters
1/2 cup white wine
2 cups sliced mushrooms
1 1/2 cups crushed tomatoes
1/2 cup heavy cream
1/4 teaspoon red pepper flakes
Salt and black pepper to taste
9 lasagna noodles, cooked al dente
1/2 cup (2 ounces) shredded Gruyère cheese
1/2 cup (2 ounces) shredded Swiss cheese
3 tablespoons chopped parsley for garnish

To prepare the béchamel sauce, melt the butter in a saucepan. Stir in the flour. Whisk in the milk. Cook until thickened, whisking constantly. Season with salt and pepper.

To prepare the lasagna, melt the butter in a skillet. Add the shallots and cook for 30 seconds. Add the shrimp and scallops. Cook until the shrimp turn pink. Add the wine. Bring to a boil. Remove the seafood with a slotted spoon and set aside. Add the mushrooms to the drippings in the skillet. Cook for 5 minutes. Stir in the béchamel sauce and tomatoes. Simmer for 5 minutes. Add the cream, red pepper flakes, salt and black pepper. Layer ingredients in a buttered 10×14-inch baking dish in the following order: sauce, 3 lasagna noodles, 1/2 seafood, sauce, 3 lasagna noodles, sauce, remaining seafood, sauce, 3 lasagna noodles, sauce and cheeses. Bake at 375 degrees for 30 minutes. Let stand before serving. Cut into squares and garnish with the parsley. **Serves 10 to 12.**

Well worth the effort.

Linguini Puttanesca with Shrimp

1/4 cup olive oil

1 tablespoon minced garlic

4 cups chopped peeled plum tomatoes, or canned imported tomatoes

1/3 cup chopped fresh parsley, divided

2 tablespoons chopped fresh basil, or 1 tablespoon dried basil

1 tablespoon oregano

1/2 teaspoon red pepper flakes, or to taste

2 tablespoons capers

18 pitted kalamata olives

2 (2-ounce) cans anchovies, drained and chopped

1 pound medium shrimp, peeled and deveined

1 pound linguini, cooked al dente

Heat the olive oil in a large saucepan. Add the garlic and cook for 30 seconds. Add the tomatoes, one-half of the parsley, the basil, oregano, red pepper flakes, capers and olives. Cook over medium-high heat for 25 minutes, stirring frequently. Add the anchovies and remaining parsley. Cook for 1 minute, stirring constantly. Add the shrimp. Cook until the shrimp turn pink. Serve over the linguini. **Serves 6.**

*Substitute twenty-four cleaned littleneck clams for the shrimp
and cook in the sauce for five minutes. Cooked chicken or turkey
may also be used. Delicious with all pasta.*

Seafood and Crab Meat Casserole

2 large eggplant, peeled and chopped
2 onions, chopped
1 green bell pepper, chopped
1/4 cup (1/2 stick) butter
2 (6-ounce) cans tomato paste
1 1/2 cups water
1/2 cup chopped green onions
1/2 cup chopped parsley
2 garlic cloves, minced
Salt to taste
Black pepper to taste
Red pepper to taste
2 pounds shrimp, peeled and deveined
1 pound crab meat, shells removed
1 cup bread crumbs
Parmesan cheese to taste

Sauté the eggplant, onions and bell pepper in the butter in a skillet until tender. Add the tomato paste and water. Simmer for 5 minutes. Add the green onions, parsley, garlic, salt, black pepper and red pepper. Cook over medium heat for 20 minutes. Add the shrimp and crab meat. Spoon into a buttered 10×15-inch baking dish. Sprinkle with the bread crumbs and Parmesan cheese. Bake at 350 degrees for 30 minutes. **Serves 8 to 10.**

This dish is better baked in advance and reheated.

Shrimp and Linguini Toss

4^1/$_2$ cups water
1^1/$_2$ pounds large shrimp
12 ounces linguini
6 ounces fresh snow peas, blanched
6 green onions, chopped
4 tomatoes, peeled and chopped
^{3}/$_4$ cup olive oil
^{1}/$_4$ cup chopped fresh parsley
^{1}/$_3$ cup wine vinegar
1 teaspoon oregano
1^1/$_2$ teaspoons basil
^{1}/$_2$ teaspoon garlic salt
^{1}/$_2$ teaspoon coarsely ground pepper

Bring the water to a boil in a large saucepan. Add the shrimp. Cook for 3 to 5 minutes or until the shrimp turn pink. Drain and rinse with cold water. Chill the shrimp. Peel and devein the shrimp. Cook the linguini using the package directions, omitting the salt. Drain and rinse with cold water. Combine the shrimp and linguini in a large bowl. Add the snow peas, green onions, tomatoes, olive oil, parsley, vinegar, oregano, basil, garlic salt and pepper and toss gently. Chill, covered, for 2 hours or longer before serving. **Serves 6 to 8.**

Stir-Fried Shrimp with Spicy Orange Sauce

1½ pounds large shrimp, peeled and deveined
1 tablespoon cornstarch
¼ cup fresh orange juice
2 tablespoons soy sauce
2 tablespoons honey
1 tablespoon rice wine vinegar
1 tablespoon chile paste with garlic
2 tablespoons canola oil
1 tablespoon minced peeled fresh ginger
3 garlic cloves, minced
⅓ cup chopped green onions
Hot cooked white rice or coconut rice

Sprinkle the shrimp with cornstarch in a bowl and toss well. Whisk the orange juice, soy sauce, honey, vinegar and chile paste in a bowl. Heat the canola oil in a nonstick skillet over medium-high heat. Add the ginger and garlic. Stir-fry for 15 seconds. Add the shrimp and stir-fry for 3 minutes. Add the orange juice mixture and green onions. Cook for 2 minutes or until the sauce thickens and the shrimp turn pink, stirring frequently. Serve immediately over white rice or coconut rice. **Serves 4.**

*Chile paste such as Sambal Oelek may be found in the
ethnic food section of your local grocery store.*

Seafood Sauces

White Cocktail Sauce
1½ tablespoons Dijon mustard
1 teaspoon Worcestershire sauce
½ teaspoon hot pepper sauce, or to taste
1 tablespoon chopped parsley
1 tablespoon horseradish
½ cup mayonnaise

Homemade Tartar Sauce
2 cups mayonnaise
2 tablespoons horseradish
2 tablespoons finely chopped onion
2 tablespoons capers
2 tablespoons sweet pickle relish
2 tablespoons chopped parsley

To prepare the white cocktail sauce, combine the Dijon mustard, Worcestershire sauce, hot sauce, parsley, horseradish and mayonnaise in a small bowl and mix well. Chill, covered, until serving time. Bring to room temperature before serving.

To prepare the homemade tartar sauce, mix the mayonnaise, horseradish, onion, capers, pickle relish and parsley in a small bowl. Store, covered, in the refrigerator. **Serves 4.**

Side Dishes

The Amelia Island lighthouse is the farthest inland of our coastal lighthouses. First constructed on Cumberland Island, Georgia, in 1820, it was moved stone by stone onto Amelia Island in 1839. It is the oldest continuously operating lighthouse in Florida and is privately maintained.

Asparagus with Cashew Butter

2 pounds fresh asparagus, trimmed
1/4 cup (1/2 stick) butter, melted
2 teaspoons fresh lemon juice
1/4 teaspoon fresh marjoram leaves
1/4 cup salted cashews, coarsely chopped

Cook the asparagus in water in a saucepan just until tender; drain. Combine the butter, lemon juice, marjoram and cashews in a small saucepan and mix well. Simmer for 2 minutes. Pour over the asparagus. **Serves 8.**

Broccoli Rabe with Prosciutto and Olives

4 tablespoons olive oil, divided
1/2 cup coarsely chopped dry bread crumbs
Salt and pepper to taste
4 ounces prosciutto, chopped
3 bunches broccoli rabe, tough stems removed
3 tablespoons fresh lemon juice
3 garlic cloves, minced
1/2 cup kalamata olives, pitted and chopped

Heat 2 tablespoons of the olive oil in a large skillet over medium heat. Add the bread crumbs. Sauté for 1 to 3 minutes or until golden brown. Sprinkle with salt and pepper. Place in a small bowl. Pour the remaining 2 tablespoons olive oil into the skillet. Add the prosciutto. Cook for 3 to 4 minutes over medium heat until light golden brown and crisp. Chop the broccoli rabe and add to the skillet. Cook for 6 to 8 minutes or until wilted completely but still bright green in color. Add the lemon juice, garlic and olives to the skillet. Cook over high heat for 2 minutes, stirring constantly. Sprinkle with salt and pepper. Remove to a warm platter. Sprinkle with the bread crumbs and serve. **Serves 6.**

Broccoli Squares

1 cup seasoned stuffing mix, divided
1/2 cup (1 stick) butter, melted
1 bunch fresh broccoli florets, blanched and chopped
1 (14-ounce) can cream-style corn
1 egg, beaten

Sauté the stuffing mix in the butter in a skillet until brown. Combine the broccoli and corn in a small bowl. Add the egg and 3/4 cup of the stuffing. Spoon into a 9×9-inch baking dish. Sprinkle with the remaining 1/4 cup stuffing. Bake at 325 degrees for 1 hour. Cut into squares to serve. **Serves 4 to 6.**

Broccoli with Lemon Cream

2 pounds fresh broccoli
6 ounces cream cheese, softened
6 tablespoons milk
1 tablespoon fresh lemon juice
1/2 teaspoon ginger
1/2 teaspoon cardamom
1 tablespoon grated lemon zest
1/2 cup sliced almonds
1 tablespoon butter

Trim the broccoli spears into 5- to 6-inch lengths. Cook the broccoli in boiling water in a saucepan just until tender; drain. Arrange two rows of broccoli in a 9×13-inch baking dish with the stems facing each other toward the center. Beat the cream cheese, milk, lemon juice, ginger and cardamom in a mixing bowl until smooth. Stir in the lemon zest. Spoon over the broccoli stems, letting the florets show. May be chilled, covered with foil, at this point. To serve, bake, uncovered, at 350 degrees for 20 to 25 minutes or until heated through. Sauté the almonds in the butter in a skillet until light brown. Sprinkle over the broccoli. **Serves 8.**

A very pretty presentation.

Brussels Sprouts and Cauliflower with Walnut Butter

2 **pounds brussels sprouts**
1 **large head cauliflower**
1/3 **cup butter**
1/2 **cup walnuts, coarsely chopped**

Trim the brussels sprouts. Cut an "X" into the stems and cut the large brussels sprouts into halves. Rinse well. Cut the cauliflower into florets. Steam the brussels sprouts and cauliflower in a steamer for 5 minutes or until tender-crisp. Drain and set aside.

Melt the butter in a Dutch oven over medium heat. Add the walnuts. Sauté for 3 minutes or until the walnuts begin to brown. Add the vegetables and toss to coat. Place in a warm serving dish. **Serves 12.**

Chilled Asparagus

2 **pounds asparagus, trimmed**
8 **teaspoons Asian sesame oil**
4 **teaspoons rice vinegar**
4 **teaspoons soy sauce**
1 **teaspoon sugar**
Salt and pepper to taste
1 **tablespoon sesame seeds, toasted**

Cook the asparagus in boiling water in a saucepan for 2 minutes or until tender-crisp. Drain and rinse with cold water. Pat the asparagus dry with paper towels and arrange on a serving platter. Whisk the sesame oil, vinegar, soy sauce, sugar, salt and pepper in a bowl until blended. Spoon over the asparagus and sprinkle with the sesame seeds. **Serves 8.**

Broccoli can be substituted for the asparagus.
The asparagus and dressing can be prepared one day in advance.
Cover each separately and chill until ready to serve.

Corn Bread Casserole

2 large onions, chopped	2 (8-ounce) packages Jiffy Corn
6 tablespoons butter	Muffin mix
2 eggs	1 cup sour cream
2 tablespoons milk	2 cups (8 ounces) shredded sharp
2 (14-ounce) cans	Cheddar cheese
cream-style corn	

Sauté the onions in the butter in a skillet until golden brown. Combine the eggs and milk in a bowl and mix well. Stir in the corn and corn muffin mix. Spread in a buttered 9×13-inch baking dish. Spoon the hot onions over the batter. Dollop the sour cream on top of the onions and spread with a fork. Sprinkle with the cheese. Bake at 425 degrees for 35 to 40 minutes or until puffed and golden brown. Let stand for 10 minutes before cutting into squares. **Serves 12 to 16.**

Great with chili. The casserole may be baked and then chilled or frozen.
To reheat, bring to room temperature and bake at 350 or 400 degrees for
10 to 15 minutes or until heated through.

Garlic and Herb Grits

4 cups water	1 cup (4 ounces) grated
4 cups milk	Parmesan cheese
1¼ teaspoons salt	4 eggs, beaten
2 cups uncooked grits	8 slices bacon, crisp-cooked
2 (6-ounce) packages Alouette	and crumbled
Garlic and Herb cheese	¼ cup chopped fresh parsley
1 teaspoon pepper	

Bring the water, milk and salt to a boil in a saucepan. Stir in the grits gradually. Return to a boil and then reduce the heat to low. Cook for 20 minutes, stirring frequently. Stir in the garlic and herb cheese, pepper and Parmesan cheese. Stir about one-fourth of the grits gradually into the eggs. Stir in the remaining grits. Pour into a lightly buttered 9×13-inch baking dish. Bake at 350 degrees for 45 to 55 minutes or until golden brown and set. Sprinkle with the parsley. Cut into squares to serve. **Serves 8 to 10.**

Green Beans Italian

1¹/2 **pounds green beans, trimmed**
1 **large onion, cut into halves and thinly sliced**
¹/4 **cup olive oil, divided**
2 **tomatoes, seeded and chopped**
¹/2 **teaspoon oregano**
Salt and pepper to taste
2 **tablespoons chopped parsley**

Cook the green beans in water in a saucepan for 5 minutes. Rinse with cold water; drain. Sauté the onion in 2 tablespoons of the olive oil in a skillet over low heat for 10 minutes or until soft but not brown. Stew the tomatoes gently in the remaining 2 tablespoons olive oil and the oregano in a saucepan until almost dry. Add the green beans and salt to the sautéed onion and lightly sauté. Add the tomato mixture and pepper and toss to mix. Heat for 5 minutes. Sprinkle with the parsley and serve immediately. **Serves 4 to 6.**

Haricots Verts with Radishes

3 **pounds haricots verts (French green beans)**
1 **cup sliced radishes**
2 **tablespoons extra-virgin olive oil**
1 **tablespoon white wine vinegar**
1 **tablespoon water**
1 **teaspoon Dijon mustard**
1 **teaspoon salt**
¹/4 **teaspoon pepper**

Steam the beans in a covered saucepan for 6 minutes or until tender-crisp. Combine the beans and radishes in a large bowl. Whisk the olive oil, vinegar, water, Dijon mustard, salt and pepper in a small bowl until blended. Drizzle over the bean mixture and toss gently. Serve immediately. **Serves 8.**

Key West Black Beans

1 pound dried black beans
12 cups water, divided
6 garlic cloves, minced
2 green bell peppers, slivered
2 large onions, chopped
2/3 cup olive oil
2 bay leaves
1 teaspoon salt
1 tablespoon vinegar
1 tablespoon sugar
2 cups cooked white rice

Bring the beans and 6 cups of the water to a boil in a Dutch oven. Boil for 2 minutes and remove from the heat. Let stand for 1 hour. Drain and rinse the beans. Return to the Dutch oven and add the remaining 6 cups water. Bring to a boil over medium-high heat. Reduce the heat to medium-low. Cook for 1½ to 2 hours. Add the garlic, bell peppers, onions, olive oil, bay leaves and salt. Cook for 1 hour. Stir in the vinegar and sugar just before serving. Discard the bay leaves. Serve over the rice. **Serves 8.**

These beans are best if cooked a day in advance. Very good served
with smoked pork chops, ham or sausage.

Mac and Three Cheeses

1 pound penne
2 cups milk
1/2 cup sour cream
2 cups heavy cream
2 teaspoons salt
2 teaspoons black pepper
2 teaspoons all-purpose flour
Dash of red pepper
1 cup (4 ounces) grated asiago cheese
1 cup (4 ounces) grated fontina cheese
1 cup (4 ounces) shredded mozzarella cheese
4 tomatoes, cut into 1/4-inch slices
1 cup fresh bread crumbs
Butter
Chopped parsley for garnish

Cook the penne using the package directions. Drain and set aside. Combine the milk, sour cream, heavy cream, salt, black pepper, flour and red pepper in a large bowl and mix well. Stir in the asiago cheese, fontina cheese and mozzarella cheese. Add the pasta and toss to mix. Spoon into a buttered 9×13-inch baking dish. Layer the tomatoes over the top. Sprinkle with the bread crumbs and dot with butter. Bake, covered with foil, at 375 degrees for 20 minutes. Bake, uncovered, for 20 minutes longer or until brown. Garnish with parsley. **Serves 10 to 12.**

Nutted Wild Rice

1¹/₂ cups wild rice 4 green onions, sliced
5 cups chicken broth ¹/₄ cup olive oil
1 cup golden raisins ¹/₃ cup orange juice
Zest of 1 orange Salt and pepper to taste
¹/₄ cup chopped fresh mint 1 cup pecan pieces, toasted

Rinse the rice. Cook in the broth in a saucepan for 40 minutes; drain. Add the raisins, orange zest, mint, green onions, olive oil and orange juice and mix well. Season with salt and pepper. Let stand for 2 hours. Stir in the pecans just before serving. **Serves 6 to 8.**

This recipe can be prepared a day in advance and chilled.
Return to room temperature when ready to serve.

Orzo with Sun-Dried Tomatoes

¹/₂ cup sun-dried tomatoes 2 teaspoons Dijon mustard
packed in oil ¹/₂ teaspoon salt
1 pound orzo ¹/₄ teaspoon pepper
4 green onions, sliced ¹/₂ cup fresh basil, cut into
¹/₄ cup red wine vinegar thin strips

Drain the sun-dried tomatoes, reserving 1 tablespoon of the oil. Coarsely chop the sun-dried tomatoes. Cook the orzo using the package directions until al dente, being careful not to overcook; drain. Combine the sun-dried tomatoes, reserved oil, green onions, vinegar, Dijon mustard, salt and pepper in a large bowl. Add the orzo and toss to coat. Let stand until slightly cool. Add the basil and toss to mix. Cover and chill if not serving immediately. **Serves 8.**

This dish can be served warm, at room temperature, or cold.

Perfect Sesame Noodles

2 tablespoons sesame oil
6 tablespoons sunflower oil
6 garlic cloves, finely chopped
2 tablespoons finely chopped fresh ginger
6 tablespoons rice wine vinegar
6 tablespoons soy sauce
1 tablespoon Chinese hot oil or chile oil
3 tablespoons sugar
1 pound vermicelli
1/2 cup chopped fresh cilantro
6 green onions, sliced
Shredded carrots

Heat the sesame oil and sunflower oil in a saucepan. Add the garlic and ginger and sauté until soft, being careful not to let the garlic or ginger become crisp or brown. Add the vinegar, soy sauce, Chinese hot oil and sugar. Boil for a few seconds and set aside. Cook the vermicelli in a saucepan until al dente; drain. Add the sauce and toss to coat well. Chill for 8 to 10 hours, tossing occasionally. Bring to room temperature before serving. Add the cilantro, green onions and carrots and toss to mix. **Serves 8.**

A perfect meal with Gingered Tuna and Bok Choy Salad.
Whole wheat linguini can be substituted for the vermicelli. You may also
substitute one teaspoon Szechuan sauce for the Chinese oil.
Copper-colored sesame oil is best.

Potato and Tomato Gratin

3 pounds Yukon Gold potatoes
Salt to taste
1/2 cup milk
1/2 cup (1 stick) butter, divided
1 cup kalamata olives, pitted and chopped
4 green onions, sliced
Pepper to taste
1 garlic clove, minced
3 cups fresh bread crumbs
1/2 cup chopped fresh parsley
1/2 cup (2 ounces) grated Parmesan cheese
3 pounds tomatoes, cut into 1/4-inch slices

Place the potatoes in a Dutch oven and cover with salted cold water. Bring to a boil. Reduce the heat and simmer for 30 minutes or until tender. Drain the potatoes. Peel the potatoes when cool enough to handle and place in a large bowl. Combine the milk and 6 tablespoons of the butter in a saucepan. Heat until the butter is melted. Cover the milk mixture and keep warm. Coarsely mash the potatoes. Fold in the milk mixture, olives, green onions, salt and pepper.

Heat the remaining 2 tablespoons butter in a nonstick skillet. Add the garlic and sauté for 1 minute. Add the bread crumbs and sauté until golden brown. Remove from the heat to cool. Stir in the parsley, cheese, salt and pepper.

Spread the potato mixture in a buttered 10×15-inch gratin dish. Cover the potatoes completely with the tomato slices. Sprinkle with the bread crumb mixture. Bake at 400 degrees on the middle oven rack for 25 minutes or until the top is golden brown and the tomatoes are tender. **Serves 6 to 8.**

The gratin can be made one day in advance. Cool completely, cover, and chill. Bring to room temperature, uncover, and reheat.

Red Cabbage

2 shallots, chopped
1/2 cup (1 stick) butter, melted
1 head red cabbage, thinly sliced
2 cups thinly sliced onions
2 Granny Smith apples, peeled and thinly sliced
3/4 cup raspberry blush vinegar
1/2 cup sugar
Salt and pepper to taste

Sauté the shallots in the butter in a large skillet for 2 minutes or until tender. Add the cabbage, onions, apples, vinegar and sugar. Cook for 15 minutes or until the cabbage is wilted, stirring frequently. Sprinkle with salt and pepper. **Serves 8.**

The cabbage can be prepared two days in advance. Cover and chill.
Reheat before serving. Excellent served with pork.

Roasted Vegetables with Orzo

1 small eggplant
2 yellow squash
2 zucchini
1 large red onion
2 garlic cloves, minced
2/3 cup olive oil, divided
1 teaspoon kosher salt, divided
1 teaspoon pepper, divided
8 ounces orzo
1/3 cup fresh lemon juice
4 green onions, finely chopped
1/4 cup pine nuts, toasted
3/4 cup (3 ounces) grated Parmesan cheese
12 fresh basil leaves, julienned

Peel the eggplant and cut into 3/4-inch slices. Cut the squash, zucchini and onion each into 1-inch chunks. Toss the eggplant, squash, zucchini, onion and garlic with 1/3 cup of the olive oil in a large bowl. Spread in a large baking pan. Sprinkle with 1/2 teaspoon of the salt and 1/2 teaspoon of the pepper. Roast at 425 degrees for 40 minutes or until brown, turning once with a spatula.

Cook the orzo using the package directions; drain. Combine the roasted vegetables with the orzo in a large bowl. Add all of the pan drippings and seasonings from the baking pan and toss to mix. Whisk the lemon juice, remaining 1/3 cup olive oil, remaining 1/2 teaspoon salt and remaining 1/2 teaspoon pepper in a bowl until blended. Pour over the pasta mixture and toss to coat. Cool to room temperature. Add the green onions, pine nuts, cheese and basil and mix well. Serve at room temperature. **Serves 6.**

Roquefort Potato Gratin

5 1/2 pounds russet potatoes
Salt and pepper to taste
2 cups whipping cream
3/4 cup crumbled Roquefort cheese
1/2 cup dry bread crumbs
1 1/2 teaspoons dried rosemary
1/4 cup (1/2 stick) butter, cut into small pieces

Peel the potatoes and cut into 1/8-inch slices. Layer in a buttered 10×15-inch baking dish, sprinkling each layer with salt and pepper. Bring the cream to a boil in a saucepan; reduce the heat. Whisk in the cheese until melted. Pour over the potatoes and cover with foil. Bake at 425 degrees for 1 hour or until the potatoes are tender. Mix the bread crumbs and rosemary in a bowl. Sprinkle over the potatoes and dot with the butter. Broil until the butter melts and the bread crumb mixture is golden brown. Let stand for 10 minutes before serving. **Serves 12.**

Spinach and Artichoke Bake

2 (10-ounce) packages frozen chopped spinach, thawed
3 tablespoons butter
1 large onion, chopped
1 (14-ounce) can quartered artichoke hearts
1 cup sour cream
Grated Parmesan cheese to taste

Cook the spinach using the package directions. Drain and squeeze dry. Melt the butter in a skillet. Add the onion and sauté until soft. Drain the artichokes and cut into smaller pieces if needed. Add to the onion and cook until the onion is translucent. Add the spinach and sour cream and mix well. Spoon into an 8×8-inch baking dish. Sprinkle with cheese. Bake at 350 degrees for 30 minutes. **Serves 4 to 6.**

*The recipe can be prepared in advance and baked when
ready to serve. For additional flavor, add one-half of an envelope
of dry onion soup mix before baking.*

Spinach-Stuffed Zucchini

3 zucchini
1 (10-ounce) package frozen chopped spinach
3 ounces cream cheese, softened
1 tablespoon horseradish
Salt to taste
1/3 cup shredded Cheddar cheese
4 slices bacon, crisp-cooked and crumbled
Several tablespoons water

Cut the zucchini lengthwise into halves. Remove the centers carefully, leaving the shells intact. Chop the centers. Cook the spinach in a saucepan using the package directions; drain well. Add the chopped zucchini, cream cheese and horseradish and mix well. Place the zucchini shells in a 9×13-inch baking dish and sprinkle with salt. Spoon the spinach mixture into the zucchini shells. Sprinkle with the cheese and bacon. Spoon the water onto the bottom of the dish. Bake at 350 degrees for 15 to 20 minutes or until tender. **Serves 6.**

The recipe can be prepared the day before and baked before serving.

Swiss Chard

1 large bunch fresh Swiss chard
2 tablespoons olive oil
1 garlic clove, sliced
Pinch of crushed red pepper
2 to 3 tablespoons water (optional)
Salt to taste
1 teaspoon butter

Rinse the Swiss chard leaves thoroughly and remove the bottom third of the stalk. Cut the leaves into 1-inch-wide strips. Heat the olive oil in a skillet over medium heat. Add the garlic and red pepper and sauté for 1 minute. Add the Swiss chard leaves. Cook, covered, for 5 minutes. Uncover and add 2 to 3 tablespoons water if the Swiss chard looks dry. Turn the leaves. Cook, covered, for 5 minutes. Remove a piece of Swiss chard and check for doneness. Continue to cook for a few minutes if needed. Sprinkle with salt and add the butter just before serving. **Serves 4.**

Turnip, Sweet Potato and Apple Casserole

3 cups turnips (1$^{1}/_{4}$ pounds)
3 cups sweet potatoes (1$^{1}/_{4}$ pounds)
2 Granny Smith apples (1$^{1}/_{4}$ pounds)
$^{2}/_{3}$ cup dried cranberries
$^{1}/_{2}$ cup packed dark brown sugar
1 tablespoon lemon juice
2 tablespoons butter, cut into small pieces

Peel the turnips, sweet potatoes and apples and cut into chunks. Combine the turnips, sweet potatoes, apples, cranberries, brown sugar and lemon juice in a buttered 2-quart baking dish. Top with the butter. Bake at 350 degrees for 1$^{1}/_{2}$ hours or until tender, stirring after 45 minutes. **Serves 12.**

Perfect for Thanksgiving or with roasted pork.

Ultimate Potato Gratin

1 (2-inch) slab bacon, cut into $1/2$-inch pieces
2 tablespoons unsalted butter, divided
4 garlic cloves, finely chopped and divided
1 head savoy cabbage, shredded
Kosher salt and pepper to taste
$1/4$ cup finely chopped fresh chives, divided
2 pounds baking potatoes, thinly sliced
$2^{1/2}$ cups heavy cream, divided
2 cups (8 ounces) grated Parmesan cheese, divided

Fry the bacon in a skillet over medium-low heat until crisp. Remove the bacon to paper towels to drain. Crumble the bacon. Add 1 tablespoon of the butter to the bacon drippings. Add one-half of the garlic and sauté until soft. Add the cabbage and remaining 1 tablespoon butter. Cook until the cabbage wilts. Stir in the bacon, salt, pepper and most of the chives. Reserve the remaining chives for garnish.

Combine the potatoes, $1^{1/2}$ cups of the cream, 1 cup of the cheese, the remaining one-half of the garlic, salt and pepper in a bowl and mix well.

Layer one-fourth of the potato mixture, $1/3$ cup of the remaining cheese and one-third of the remaining potato mixture in a buttered 10×15-inch baking dish. Spread the cabbage mixture evenly over the layers. Continue layering with one-half of the remaining potato mixture, $1/3$ cup of the remaining cheese and the remaining potato mixture. Pour the remaining 1 cup cream over the top. Sprinkle with the remaining $1/3$ cup cheese. Bake, covered with foil, at 375 degrees for 1 hour. Bake, uncovered, for 30 minutes longer or until golden brown. Let stand for 10 minutes before serving. Garnish with the reserved remaining chives. **Serves 6 to 8.**

Endings

On Amelia Island, life seems to be lived at a slower pace. Southern hospitality
prevails in this nature lover's paradise. Pull up a chair and enjoy the incredible sunsets
ranging in red and orange colors that illuminate the western sky. We watch
with wonder the sun's final moments and savor the ending of another perfect day.

Apple-Pecan Cake with Caramel Sauce

1 cup all-purpose flour

1 teaspoon baking soda

1/2 teaspoon kosher salt

1/2 teaspoon cinnamon

1/2 teaspoon ginger

1/4 teaspoon ground allspice

1/4 teaspoon nutmeg

1/8 teaspoon ground cloves

3/4 cup (1 1/2 sticks) unsalted butter, softened and divided

1 1/4 cups granulated sugar, divided

1 egg, beaten

2 Granny Smith apples, peeled and chopped

1/2 cup chopped pecans

1/4 cup heavy cream

1/4 cup packed dark brown sugar

1/2 teaspoon vanilla extract

Mix the flour, baking soda, salt, cinnamon, ginger, allspice, nutmeg and cloves together. Cream 1/2 cup of the butter, 1 cup of the granulated sugar and the egg in a mixing bowl. Add the flour mixture and beat well. Stir in the apples and pecans. Spread evenly in a buttered 9×9-inch glass baking dish. Bake at 350 degrees for 45 minutes.

Combine the cream, remaining 1/4 cup butter, remaining 1/4 cup granulated sugar and the brown sugar in a saucepan. Cook until the granulated sugar and brown sugar dissolve. Stir in the vanilla. Cut the cake into squares and top with the caramel sauce. **Serves 6 to 8.**

Warm the cake and the sauce before serving if made in advance.

Chocolate Cherry Cake

1 box Duncan Hines butter fudge cake mix
2 eggs, beaten
2 teaspoons almond extract
1 (21-ounce) can Comstock cherry pie filling
1 cup sugar
1/3 cup milk
5 tablespoons butter
1 cup (6 ounces) semisweet chocolate morsels
1 teaspoon vanilla extract
Maraschino cherries with stems

Combine the cake mix, eggs and almond extract in a bowl and mix with a fork. Do not use an electric mixer. Stir in the pie filling. Spread evenly in a lightly buttered and floured 10×15-inch cake pan or two 8×8-inch cake pans. Bake at 350 degrees for 30 minutes. Cool in the cake pan for 30 minutes before removing.

Bring the sugar, milk and butter to a boil in a saucepan. Boil for 1 minute and remove from the heat. Add the chocolate morsels and stir until smooth. Stir in the vanilla. Pour over the cooled cake.

To serve, cut the cake into squares and place each square on a flattened cupcake liner. Top each with a maraschino cherry. **Serves 24.**

Great for a crowd. If preparing cupcakes, bake for only 15 minutes.
Any chocolate cake mix can be used in this recipe.

Cocoa Buttermilk Cake

Cake
2¹/₃ cups all-purpose flour
³/₄ cup unsweetened cocoa powder
1 teaspoon baking soda
³/₄ teaspoon baking powder
¹/₂ teaspoon salt
³/₄ cup (1¹/₂ sticks) butter, softened
1 cup granulated sugar
1 cup packed brown sugar
3 eggs, at room temperature
2 teaspoons vanilla extract
1¹/₂ cups buttermilk

Mascarpone Frosting
4 ounces mascarpone cheese, softened
¹/₂ cup (1 stick) butter, softened
¹/₃ cup unsweetened cocoa powder
2 tablespoons (or more) milk
2 teaspoons vanilla extract
1 (1-pound) package confectioners' sugar, sifted

To prepare the cake, lightly butter and flour the bottoms of three 8-inch cake pans. Line the bottoms with waxed paper. Lightly butter and flour the waxed paper and sides of the pans. Mix the flour, cocoa, baking soda, baking powder and salt in a bowl. Cream the butter in a mixing bowl. Add the granulated sugar and brown sugar gradually, beating constantly. Beat at medium speed for 2 minutes. Add the eggs one at a time, beating well after each addition. Stir in the vanilla. Add the flour mixture and buttermilk alternately, beating at low speed after each addition until combined. Spread in the prepared pans. Bake at 350 degrees for 30 to 35 minutes or until a wooden pick inserted in the center comes out clean. Cool in the pans for 10 minutes. Invert onto wire racks to cool completely.

To prepare the frosting, beat the mascarpone cheese, butter, cocoa, milk and vanilla in a mixing bowl until creamy. Add the confectioners' sugar gradually, beating constantly until smooth. Add additional milk 1 teaspoon at a time if needed for the desired spreading consistency. Spread between the layers and over the top and side of the cake.
Serves 12 to 16.

Coconut Chocolate Cheesecake

1¹/₂ cups chocolate wafer cookie crumbs (28 to 30 cookies)

3 tablespoons sugar

¹/₄ cup (¹/₂ stick) butter, melted

32 ounces cream cheese, softened

3 eggs

1 cup sugar

1 (14-ounce) package flaked coconut

1 (11-ounce) package milk chocolate morsels

¹/₂ cup slivered almonds, toasted

1 teaspoon vanilla extract

¹/₂ cup (3 ounces) semisweet chocolate morsels

Toasted chopped almonds

Mix the cookie crumbs, 3 tablespoons sugar and the butter in a bowl. Press over the bottom of a 10-inch springform pan. Bake at 350 degrees for 8 minutes. Cool on a wire rack. Maintain the oven temperature. Beat the cream cheese, eggs and 1 cup sugar in a mixing bowl until fluffy. Stir in the coconut, milk chocolate morsels, ¹/₂ cup slivered almonds and the vanilla. Pour over the crust. Bake for 1 hour. Remove from the oven and cool on a wire rack for 1 hour. Place the semisweet chocolate morsels in a sealable plastic bag and seal. Submerge the bag in hot water until the chocolate morsels melt. Cut a tiny hole in one corner of the bag and drizzle the chocolate over the cheesecake. Sprinkle with chopped almonds. Chill until the chocolate is firm. Cover with plastic wrap and chill for 8 hours before serving. **Serves 12.**

The cheesecake can be stored, covered with plastic wrap, in the refrigerator for up to five days.

Creamy Cheesecake

3/4 cup graham cracker crumbs

2 tablespoons sugar

2 tablespoons butter, softened

4 eggs

1 cup sugar

24 ounces cream cheese, cut into cubes and softened

1 teaspoon vanilla extract

2 teaspoons fresh lemon juice

1 cup sour cream

1/4 cup sugar

2 ounces sliced almonds

Lightly butter the side and bottom of a 9-inch springform pan. Mix the graham cracker crumbs, 2 tablespoons sugar and the butter in a bowl until crumbly. Press over the bottom and up the side to within 1 inch of the rim of the springform pan. Process the eggs and 1 cup sugar in a blender until blended. Add the cream cheese gradually, blending until light in color and smooth. Add the vanilla and lemon juice and blend well. Pour gradually into the crust. Bake at 350 degrees for 30 to 35 minutes or until the cheesecake begins to pull away from the crust and cracks slightly around the edge. The center should appear slightly undercooked at the end of baking. Do not overbake.

Combine the sour cream and 1/4 cup sugar in a bowl and mix well. Spread over the hot cheesecake. Sprinkle with the almonds. Broil on the middle oven rack for 1 minute or until the almonds are light golden brown. Cool on a wire rack. Chill, covered, in the refrigerator. **Serves 12.**

*A can of cherry or blueberry pie filling may be used as a topping
on the cooled cheesecake instead of the sour cream topping.*

Date-Nut Cake with Orange Glaze

3 cups all-purpose flour
1¹/₃ teaspoons baking soda
¹/₂ teaspoon salt
¹/₂ cup (1 stick) butter, softened
1¹/₂ cups sugar, divided
2 eggs
1 cup buttermilk
1 cup chopped dates
1 cup chopped pecans
¹/₂ cup shredded coconut
1 teaspoon vanilla extract
²/₃ cup fresh orange juice
2 tablespoons orange zest
Whipped cream (optional)

Mix the flour, baking soda and salt together. Cream the butter and ¹/₂ cup of the sugar in a large mixing bowl. Add the eggs and beat well. Add the flour mixture and buttermilk alternately, beating well after each addition. Stir in the dates, pecans, coconut and vanilla. Pour into a buttered 9×13-inch baking dish. Bake at 300 degrees for 45 minutes.

Combine the orange juice, orange zest and remaining 1 cup sugar in a bowl and mix well. Pour over the hot cake. Top with whipped cream. **Serves 12.**

*Blend 1 tablespoon vinegar into 1 cup milk to use
as a substitute for the buttermilk.*

Holiday Pumpkin Roll

1¼ cups confectioners' sugar, divided
¾ cup all-purpose flour
½ teaspoon baking powder
½ teaspoon baking soda
1½ teaspoons cinnamon
1 teaspoon pumpkin pie spice
½ teaspoon nutmeg
¼ teaspoon salt
3 eggs
1 cup granulated sugar
⅔ cup canned pumpkin
1 cup chopped walnuts
8 ounces cream cheese, softened
6 tablespoons butter, softened
1 teaspoon vanilla extract

Spray a jelly roll pan with nonstick baking spray. Line the pan with buttered and floured waxed paper. Sprinkle a towel with ¼ cup of the confectioners' sugar. Mix the flour, baking powder, baking soda, cinnamon, pumpkin pie spice, nutmeg and salt in a small bowl. Beat the eggs and granulated sugar in a large bowl until thick. Stir in the pumpkin. Add the flour mixture and mix well. Spread evenly in the prepared jelly roll pan. Sprinkle with the walnuts. Bake at 375 degrees for 13 to 15 minutes or until the cake tests done. Loosen the cake from the side of the pan and invert onto the prepared towel. Peel off the waxed paper. Roll up the cake in the towel. Cool on a wire rack.

Beat the cream cheese, the remaining 1 cup confectioners' sugar, the butter and vanilla in a small mixing bowl until smooth. Unroll the cake and remove the towel. Spread the cream cheese mixture over the cake and roll up to enclose the filling. Wrap in plastic wrap and chill until serving time. **Serves 15.**

One fifteen-ounce can pumpkin makes two rolls.
Wrap the rolls in foil and freeze.

Lemonade Cake

Cake
2¼ cups cake flour

1¾ cups sugar

1 tablespoon baking powder

1 teaspoon salt

½ cup vegetable oil

½ cup lemonade

5 egg yolks

¼ cup fresh lemon juice

1 tablespoon grated lemon zest

1 cup egg whites (whites of 7 or 8 eggs)

½ teaspoon cream of tartar

Lemon Glaze
1 cup confectioners' sugar

1 tablespoon fresh lemon juice

½ teaspoon grated lemon zest

1 teaspoon lemonade

To prepare the cake, spray a 10-inch tube pan with a removable bottom with nonstick baking spray or butter and flour the pan. Sift the cake flour, sugar, baking powder and salt into a bowl and make a well in the center. Add the oil, lemonade, egg yolks, lemon juice and lemon zest and whisk until smooth. Beat the egg whites and cream of tartar in a mixing bowl until stiff but not dry. Fold into the batter one-fourth at a time. Bake at 325 degrees for 55 minutes or until golden brown on top. Invert onto a bottle and cool. Remove the cake from the pan and place on a cake plate.

To prepare the glaze, whisk the confectioners' sugar, lemon juice, lemon zest and lemonade in a bowl until thick. Drizzle over the cooled cake. Store at room temperature. **Serves 12.**

Butter Sugar Cookies

1 cup granulated sugar	2 teaspoons vanilla extract
1 cup confectioners' sugar	1/2 teaspoon almond extract
1 cup (2 sticks) butter, softened	1 teaspoon baking soda
1 cup vegetable oil	1 teaspoon cream of tartar
2 eggs	1/4 teaspoon salt
5 cups all-purpose flour	Additional granulated sugar

Cream 1 cup granulated sugar, the confectioners' sugar, butter and oil in a mixing bowl. Add the eggs, flour, vanilla, almond extract, baking soda, cream of tartar and salt and mix well. Chill, covered, for 8 to 10 hours. Roll into balls or drop by rounded teaspoonfuls onto an ungreased Teflon baking sheet. Press down with a flat-bottomed glass dipped in additional granulated sugar to flatten very thin. Crisscross with the tines of a fork. Bake at 350 degrees for 6 to 8 minutes or until the edges are light brown. Cool on a wire rack. **Makes 5 dozen.**

*The secret is to make these cookies as thin as possible. For a festive
look, red and green sugar may be used at Christmas. Use a Waterford
glass for a design as you flatten the cookies.*

Chocolate Marshmallow Brownies

4 ounces unsweetened chocolate squares	1/8 teaspoon salt
	2 teaspoons vanilla extract
1 cup (2 sticks) butter	2 cups (12 ounces) semisweet chocolate morsels
2 cups sugar	
4 eggs	2 cups miniature marshmallows
1 cup all-purpose flour	

Melt the unsweetened chocolate and butter in a saucepan over medium-high heat, stirring constantly. Add the sugar. Heat until the sugar dissolves, stirring constantly. Cool for 15 minutes. Add the eggs and stir until blended. Add the flour, salt and vanilla and mix well. Fold in the chocolate morsels and marshmallows. Spoon into a buttered 9×13-inch baking pan. Bake at 325 degrees for 30 to 35 minutes or until the brownies pull from the sides of the pan. Cool in the pan on a wire rack. Cover and let stand at room temperature for 8 to 10 hours before cutting into squares. **Serves 24.**

Cranberry Oatmeal Cookies

2/3 cup all-purpose flour	2/3 cup granulated sugar
1/2 teaspoon salt	2/3 cup packed light brown sugar
1/2 teaspoon baking soda	1 egg
1/2 cup old-fashioned oats	1 teaspoon vanilla extract
3/4 cup (1 1/2 sticks) unsalted butter, softened	2 cups chopped pecans
	1 cup dried cranberries

Mix the flour, salt and baking soda in a bowl. Stir in the oats. Cream the butter, granulated sugar and brown sugar in a mixing bowl until light and fluffy. Add the egg and beat well. Add the vanilla and the flour mixture and mix well. Stir in the pecans and cranberries. Shape into 1 1/4-inch balls and place on a cookie sheet. Bake at 350 degrees for 9 minutes or until lacy and golden brown. Cool completely on a wire rack. Remove to a serving plate. **Makes 3 dozen.**

Everyone agrees these cookies are the best. The cookies may be stored in an airtight container for up to one week and up to one month in the freezer. As a variation, 1/2 cup chocolate morsels can be added.

Killer Brownies

4 ounces unsweetened chocolate	1 1/2 cups sugar
2 ounces semisweet chocolate	2/3 cup all-purpose flour
1 cup (2 sticks) butter	1 teaspoon vanilla extract
3 eggs	Dash of salt

Place the unsweetened chocolate, semisweet chocolate and butter in a microwave-safe bowl. Microwave at 50 percent power until melted, stirring at 30-second intervals. Beat the eggs and sugar in a mixing bowl until light. Stir in the chocolate mixture, flour, vanilla and salt. Spread in a buttered 9×9-inch baking pan. Bake at 350 degrees for 30 to 35 minutes or until the brownies begin to pull away from the sides of the pan. Cool on a wire rack. Cut into squares. **Serves 9.**

To die for!

Minted Chocolate Delights

3 cups all-purpose flour	2 eggs
1¼ teaspoons baking soda	⅓ cup butter, softened
1⅛ teaspoons salt, divided	3 cups confectioners'
¾ cup (1½ sticks) butter	sugar, divided
1½ cups packed brown sugar	⅛ teaspoon peppermint extract
2 tablespoons water or red wine	¼ cup milk or light cream
2 cups (12 ounces) semisweet	
chocolate morsels	

Mix the flour, baking soda and 1 teaspoon of the salt together. Melt ¾ cup butter with the brown sugar in a saucepan over low heat, stirring frequently. Remove from the heat. Stir in the water and chocolate morsels until melted. Beat in the eggs. Add the flour mixture gradually, stirring well after each addition. Drop by generous teaspoonfuls onto a buttered cookie sheet. Bake at 350 degrees for 8 to 10 minutes or until set. Cool on a wire rack. Beat ⅓ cup butter, 1 cup of the confectioners' sugar, the remaining ⅛ teaspoon salt and the peppermint extract in a mixing bowl until fluffy. Add the remaining 2 cups confectioners' sugar alternately with the milk, beating constantly. Spread over the cooled cookies. **Makes 4 dozen.**

*The cookies can be sandwiched together with one rounded teaspoon
of the frosting in the middle.*

Molasses Cookies

4½ cups all-purpose flour	1½ cups shortening
4 teaspoons baking soda	2 cups sugar
1 teaspoon ground cloves	½ cup molasses
1 teaspoon ginger	2 eggs
2 teaspoons cinnamon	Sugar for rolling
1 teaspoon salt	

Sift the flour, baking soda, cloves, ginger, cinnamon and salt together. Melt the shortening in a saucepan over low heat. Remove from the heat and cool completely. Add 2 cups sugar, the molasses and eggs and beat well. Add the flour mixture and mix well. The batter will be stiff. Chill for 3 hours or longer. Shape into balls and roll in sugar. Place on a cookie sheet lined with baking parchment. Bake at 375 degrees for 8 to 10 minutes or until set. Cool on a wire rack. **Makes 6 dozen.**

Oatmeal and Chocolate Squares

3 cups quick-cooking oats
2¹/₂ cups all-purpose flour
1 teaspoon baking soda
1¹/₂ teaspoons salt, divided
1 cup (2 sticks) butter, softened
2 cups packed brown sugar
2 eggs
4 teaspoons vanilla extract, divided
1 (14-ounce) can sweetened condensed milk
1¹/₂ cups (9 ounces) semisweet chocolate morsels
2 tablespoons butter
¹/₂ cup chopped walnuts or shredded coconut

Mix the oats, flour, baking soda and 1 teaspoon of the salt in a bowl. Cream 1 cup butter and the brown sugar in a large mixing bowl. Beat in the eggs and 2 teaspoons of the vanilla. Stir in the oat mixture. Heat the condensed milk, chocolate morsels, 2 tablespoons butter and the remaining ¹/₂ teaspoon salt in a saucepan over low heat until smooth. Remove from the heat. Stir in the walnuts and remaining 2 teaspoons vanilla. Pat two-thirds of the oat mixture in a buttered 9×13-inch baking dish. Spread the chocolate mixture over the top. Cover with the remaining oat mixture. Bake at 350 degrees for 30 minutes or until light brown. Cool and cut into small squares. **Makes 50 squares.**

Angel Chocolate Pie

3 egg whites, at room temperature	4 ounces Baker's German's sweet chocolate
1/8 teaspoon salt	3 tablespoons water
1/8 teaspoon cream of tartar	1 cup heavy whipping cream
3/4 cup plus 1 tablespoon sugar	Chocolate sauce
1 3/4 teaspoons vanilla extract, divided	Whipped cream for garnish
1/2 cup finely chopped pecans, toasted	

Beat the egg whites with the salt and cream of tartar at high speed in a mixing bowl until soft peaks form. Add 3/4 cup of the sugar 2 tablespoons at a time, beating constantly until stiff peaks form. Fold in 3/4 teaspoon of the vanilla and the pecans. Spoon into a lightly buttered 9-inch pie plate and shape into a nest-like shell, building up the side above the edge of the pie plate. Bake at 300 degrees for 50 to 55 minutes or until golden brown. Cool on a wire rack. Place the chocolate and water in a microwave-safe bowl. Microwave, covered, on High for 30 seconds. Stir until the chocolate is melted. Cool until thickened. Whip the whipping cream, remaining 1 teaspoon vanilla and the remaining 1 tablespoon sugar in a bowl until firm peaks form. Fold into the chocolate mixture. Spoon into the meringue shell. Chill for 2 hours. Cut into slices. Place on serving plates drizzled with chocolate sauce and garnished with whipped cream. **Serves 6 to 8.**

Easy Piecrust

1 1/2 cups all-purpose flour	1/2 cup vegetable oil
2 teaspoons sugar	2 tablespoons milk
1 teaspoon salt	

Sift the flour, sugar and salt into a 9-inch pie plate. Blend the oil and milk in a small bowl. Pour over the flour mixture and mix with a fork. Press into the pie plate and flute the edge. Add your favorite pie filling and bake as directed in the recipe. **Makes 1 crust.**

Never fails and is always perfect.

Fancy Frozen Lemon Pie

1/4 cup (1/2 stick) butter, softened
1/2 cup packed brown sugar
1 1/2 cups crushed Total cereal
1/2 cup chopped walnuts
3 eggs, separated and
at room temperature

1/2 cup granulated sugar
1 cup heavy whipping cream
1/4 cup fresh lemon juice
1 teaspoon grated lemon zest

Bring the butter and brown sugar just to the boiling point in a saucepan over low heat. Cook for 1 minute longer and remove from the heat. Stir in the cereal and walnuts. Spread on a rimmed baking sheet and cool completely. Beat the egg whites at high speed in a medium mixing bowl until soft peaks form. Add the granulated sugar gradually, beating constantly until stiff peaks form. Beat the egg yolks in a mixing bowl until thick. Fold into the meringue. Beat the whipping cream and lemon juice in a mixing bowl until firm peaks form. Stir in the lemon zest. Fold into the egg mixture.

Crumble the cereal mixture. Line a buttered 9-inch pie plate with 2 cups of the cereal mixture to form a shell. Spoon the lemon filling into the pie shell. Sprinkle the top with the remaining cereal mixture. Freeze for 6 to 8 hours or until firm. Remove from the freezer and let stand for 15 to 20 minutes before serving. This recipe contains raw egg. **Serves 12.**

Frozen Turtle Dessert

17 ice cream sandwiches, divided
1 (12-ounce) jar caramel topping
1 1/2 cups chopped pecans, toasted and divided
12 ounces frozen whipped topping, thawed and divided
3/4 cup hot fudge topping, heated

Place 8 1/2 of the ice cream sandwiches in a 9×13-inch dish. Spread with the caramel topping. Sprinkle with 1 cup of the pecans. Spread 2 cups of the whipped topping over the layers. Continue layering with the remaining ice cream sandwiches and remaining whipped topping. Sprinkle with the remaining 1/2 cup pecans. Freeze, covered, for 2 hours or longer. Let stand for 5 minutes before serving. Cut into squares. Drizzle with the warm hot fudge topping before serving. Kids adore this, and it is easy enough for them to help assemble. **Serves 10.**

Lemon Pudding Soufflé with Strawberry Coulis

Strawberry Coulis
1 pint fresh strawberries, sliced
1/4 cup orange juice
3 tablespoons sugar
1 teaspoon balsamic vinegar

Soufflé
3 tablespoons butter, softened
1 cup sugar
4 eggs, separated and divided
1/2 cup fresh lemon juice
1/4 teaspoon salt
3 tablespoons all-purpose flour
1 cup milk

To prepare the strawberry coulis, purée the strawberries in a blender. Press firmly through a sieve and reserve the solids. Bring the orange juice and sugar to a boil in a medium saucepan, stirring constantly until the sugar dissolves. Remove from the heat. Stir in the balsamic vinegar and reserved solids. Pour into a serving bowl and cool completely. Chill in the refrigerator.

To prepare the soufflé, cream the butter and sugar in a mixing bowl until fluffy. Add the egg yolks and mix well. Add the lemon juice, salt and flour and beat well. Stir in the milk until blended. Beat the egg whites at high speed in a mixing bowl until stiff peaks form. Fold into the lemon mixture. Pour into a lightly buttered 6-cup soufflé dish. Bake at 325 degrees for 50 minutes, covering with foil during the last 10 minutes if the top begins to overbrown. Spoon into serving bowls. Serve warm or chilled with the strawberry coulis. **Serves 6.**

The coulis is good served on waffles, pound cake, or ice cream. The coulis can be prepared well in advance and chilled until ready to use.

Lotus Ice Cream

1/2 cup slivered almonds	3 cups half-and-half
3 lemons	8 sprigs of fresh mint
1 1/2 cups sugar	for garnish

Spread the almonds on a baking sheet. Bake at 350 degrees for 6 to 8 minutes or until toasted. Let stand until cool.

Grate the zest from the lemons into a bowl. Squeeze the juice from the lemons over the lemon zest. Add the sugar and stir until dissolved. Stir in the half-and-half gradually. Pour into an ice cream freezer container. Freeze using the ice cream freezer directions until the ice cream begins to thicken. Add the toasted almonds. Continue to freeze until firm. Spoon into stemmed glasses. Garnish each with a sprig of mint. **Serves 8.**

Not your ordinary ice cream. This is very special.

Pumpkin Squares

1 (15-ounce) can pumpkin	1/2 gallon vanilla ice cream,
1 cup sugar	softened
1 teaspoon salt	36 gingersnaps
1 teaspoon ginger	1 cup heavy whipping cream,
1/2 teaspoon nutmeg	whipped
1 teaspoon cinnamon	18 pecan halves
1 cup chopped pecans, toasted	

Combine the pumpkin, sugar, salt, ginger, nutmeg and cinnamon in a bowl and mix well. Stir in the chopped pecans. Fold into the softened ice cream in a chilled bowl. Line the bottom of a 9×13-inch dish with one-half of the gingersnaps. Layer with one-half of the ice cream mixture, the remaining gingersnaps and the remaining ice cream mixture. Freeze until firm. Cut into squares to serve. Top each square with the whipped cream and a pecan half. **Serves 18.**

Notes

Cookbook Development Committee

Chairs

Carol Filbert
Nancy Jones

Cookbook Committee

Barbara Bookman
Sue Braddock
Cheryl Donaldson
Betty Lee
Iris Nicholson
Sandy Shaw

Art Director

Iris Jacobsen

Photographers

Max Hertweck
Robie Ray

Marketing Committee

Dickie Anderson
Katey Breen
Elaine Coats
Maryellen Covallo
Jan Davis
Anne Entriken
Peggy Harlow
Linda Marshall

Tara Meyer-Robson
Patti Montgomery
Gail Morgan
Judith Pines
Claire Salmond
Krista Saye
Marie Smith

Contributors and Testers

A special thank-you to all who contributed to the success of this endeavor. We salute the culinary talents of our many friends who shared their favorite recipes. We thank those individuals who tested recipes. Although we could not include every recipe, we appreciate your interest and generosity in supporting Micah's Place. It is our hope that no name has been inadvertently overlooked.

The staff, board of directors, and auxiliary of Micah's Place also thank you for your support in our continued fund-raising efforts to prevent domestic violence and help its victims.

Katherine Abraham	Cheryl Broome **	Carol Filbert **
Gloria Adams	Anne Bundy	Jane Flynn
Anne Allen **	Mimi Byrnes	Josephine Francesconi
Ann Adele Allf	Vicki Callan	Maddy Franchi
Dickie Anderson	Becky Carter	Cheryl Gardner
Marge Andreason	Mary Lou Casagrande	Mary Lee Garrett
Carol Ann Atwood	Betsy Chapman	Pat Gieg
Andrea Bardusch	Elaine Coats **	Vera Gordinier
Sue Bartholomae	Anne Coonrod	Tuck Gordon
Irene Basore	Pat Corbin	Marie Grant
Sylvie Baxter **	Linda Coughlin	Clark Griffin-Eddings
Polly Benninghoff	Freddy Cox	Anne Hammer
Jody Best	Sherry Crandall	Shirley Hargreaves
Joan Betts	Frances Davis	Margie Harkins
Jim Bird	Jan Davis	Karen Harper
Julie Blake	Laura DeLong	Lisa Harter
Barbara Bookman **	Mary Ann DiBlasio	Julie Lee Hatton
Leah Bork	Noreen Dionne	Janet Hayes
Rosalind Bowles	Cheryl Donaldson **	Phyllis Helmes
Lillie Bowman	Trish Dooley	Sally Henderson **
Sheila Braddock **	Jen Duhy	Queet Hertweck **
Sue Braddock **	Joan Duncan	Delores Higginbotham
Russell Bradshaw	Fran Erbrick	Cynthia Holler **
Mary Brannen	Amy Filbert	Phyllis Holmes

Penny Holst
Barrie Hooley
Carol Howard
Gael Hoysgaard
Janet Hughes
Pris Jackson
David Jacobsen
Iris Jacobsen
Betty Jensen
Tess Johnson
D. J. Johnston
Barbara Jones
Nancy Jones
Nancy R. Jones **
Jean Kailey
Sandy Karlovec
Barbie Keith
Susie Kirk
Diane Kirtley
Peggy Kiser
Janet Kolar **
Marie Korta
Lois Laing
Vicki Lanier
Betty Lee **
Dan Lee
John Lee
Pam Lee
Susan Little
Debbie Lott
Diane MacDonell
Frank Malone
Mickey Martin
Sharon Martin
Kay McCaffrey
Marion McCully
Diane McDonald

Barbara McGinley
Ed McGinley
Jan McGraw
Llona Meaux
Ronnie Melnick
Bill Merman
Jo Merman
Lynn Meyer **
Kathy Miller
Donna Mitchell
Eileen Shannon Moore
Jean Evans Morgan
Sally Ann Morris
Marlene Murphy
Elaine Nelson
Iris Nicholson **
Frances Orton
Diane Pasieka
Dottie Perry
Judy Pillans
Teresa Pratt
Dana Preik
Jennifer Preik **
Jane Preston
Pat Price
JonAnna Reidinger
Rose Rigdon
Molly Rinehart
Bill Rion
Lyn Rion
Flo Rives
Salli Roberts **
Deborah Rollins
Mary Ruark
Marianne Salas
Nan Sands
Gail Sasanfar

Alexandra Sayre
Sis Schalon
Elizabeth Scheibert
Audrey Lincourt Schiebler
Eileen Searle
Roberta Selzer
Sandy Shaw **
Jo Shepherd
Pam Simmons
Carol Simon
Chef Bernhard Smit
Laura Smith
Gary Snyder
Mary Jane Spellman
Ed Sproat
Sandy Sproat
Lynne Stafford
Patsy Stegall
Beverly Stormoen
Nina Suddath
Carol Tarpenning
Gina Taylor
Margaret Thompson
Pat vanAmerongen
Gail Villani
Nancie Waldron
Carol Weldon
Wendy Wessels
Sara Wight
Joyce Williams
Paige Williams
Jane Wilson
Betty Wolfe
Lindy Wyman
Dora Yelk
Jan Young
** Denotes recipe testers

Index

A Savory Place

Culinary Favorites of Amelia Island

Micah's Place
P.O. Box 16287
Fernandina Beach, Florida 32035
development@micahsplace.org
904-491-6364
www.micahsplace.org

YOUR ORDER	QUANTITY	TOTAL
A Savory Place at $24.95 per book		$
Shipping and handling at $4.95 for one book; $2.00 for each additional book to same address		$
	TOTAL	$

Name

Address

City   State   Zip

Telephone   E-mail

Method of Payment: [   ] MasterCard   [   ] VISA   [   ] Check payable to Micah's Place

Credit Card Number   Expiration Date

Signature

Cookbooks are also available at www.micahsplace.org.

Micah's Place is a 501(c)(3) nonprofit organization and provides prevention and intervention services to victims of domestic violence.